July 8th, 1913, St. Louis, Missouri

"Many moons ago I Lived. Again I come Patience Worth my name."

The two women, twenty-one year old Pearl Curran and her friend Emily Hutchings, gasped and stared at each other. The planchette started moving again and spelled out:

"Wait, I would speak with thee. If thou shalt live, then so shall I. I make my bread by thy hearth. Good friends, let us be merrie. The time for work is past. Let the tabbie drowse and blink her wisdom into the fire-log."

Into the Light

When you hear the terms *ouija board, table-tipping, séance, medium*, or *channeler*, they may conjure up a host of emotions: interest, amusement, derision...even unease. Much talked about—yet seldom explained—the subject of the spirit world is a recipe for strong emotions in most.

In *Spirit Guides & Angel Guardians*, Richard Webster takes us through time and back again—exploring the history and beliefs behind these mysterious apparitions. He dispels many of the fears and misconceptions connected with the spirit world, and teaches us how to make contact with our own guides.

This book represents the culmination of the author's life-long fascination with spirit guides and angel guardians. It is deeply rooted in his own experiences, and also contains numerous accounts from people who consult with their own guides daily.

About the Author

Richard Webster was born in New Zealand in 1946, where he still resides. He travels widely every year, lecturing and conducting workshops on psychic subjects around the world. He has written many books, mainly on psychic subjects, and also writes monthly magazine columns.

Richard is married with three children. His family is very supportive of his occupation, but his oldest son, after watching his father's career, has decided to become an accountant.

Many of Llewellyn's authors have websites with additional information and resources. For more information, please visit our website at www.llewellyn.com.

Contact Your Invisible Helpers

SPIRIT GUIDES & ANGEL GUARDIANS

Richard Webster

2004
Llewellyn Publications
St. Paul, Minnesota 55164-0383

Cover design: Michelle Dilley
Cover photo: Cowgirl Stock Photography
Editing and layout: Cathy Taylor
Book design and project management: Amy Rost

FIRST EDITION
Twelfth Printing, 2004

Library of Congress Cataloging In-Publication Data
Webster, Richard, 1946–
Spirit guides & angel guardians : contact your invisible helpers / Richard Webster. — 1st ed.
p. cm.
Includes bibliographical references and index.
ISBN 1-56718-795-1 (trade paper)
1. Guides (Spiritualism) 2. Guardian angels. I. Title.
BF1275.G85W34 1998
133.9—dc21 97-52675
CIP

Llewellyn Publications
A Division of Llewellyn Worldwide, Ltd.
P.O. Box 64383, Dept. 1-56718-795-1
St. Paul, MN 55164-0383, U.S.A.
www.llewellyn.com

Printed in the United States of America

Other Books by Richard Webster

(Published by Llewellyn Publications)

101 Feng Shui Tips for the Home
(first of the Feng Shui Series)

Astral Travel for Beginners

Aura Reading for Beginners

Seven Secrets to Success

Feng Shui for Beginners

Dowsing for Beginners

Numerology Magic

Omens, Oghams & Oracles

Chinese Numerology

Feng Shui for Apartment Living

Feng Shui for the Workplace

Feng Shui for Love and Romance

Feng Shui in the Garden

Feng Shui for Success & Happiness

Palm Reading for Beginners

Soul Mates

Success Secrets

The Complete Book of Palmistry (formerly *Revealing Hands*)

Practical Guide to Past-Life Memories

Write Your Own Magic

Pendulum Magic for Beginners

Is Your Pet Psychic?

Playing Card Divination for Beginners

How to Write for the New Age Market

Dedication

For Penny,
our family's guardian angel.

Contents

Part Two: Spirit Guides

Preface

I have found the assistance of guardian angels and spirit guides to be invaluable in my own life. Every now and again, over the years, I have had the opportunity to help people make contact with their guides or angels and they have all benefited from this. My purpose in writing this book is to introduce many more people to the spirit world than I can on a one-to-one basis.

There is a great deal of confusion about spirit guides and guardian angels. Some people claim that they are one and the same. This is not surprising, as spirit guides can sometimes appear in the form of angels. However, there is a considerable difference between the two, and I wanted this book to make the distinction clear.

You will find your spiritual and personal growth will take a huge leap forward as soon as you welcome your guardian angels and guides into your life. I have been privileged in seeing this happen to many people, and the changes that occur are a joy to behold.

You will experience more fun, happiness, and fulfillment in your life than ever before. Other people will notice the difference in you as well, as you will become calmer, more relaxed and much more loving than ever before. Your love for yourself, family, friends, and humanity in general will expand, enhancing every area of your life.

We all have problems at times. No matter how difficult your life may be, you will find your progress smoother, calmer, and faster when you allow your spirit guides and angel guardians to help you.

Introduction

Your Unlimited Potential

What would your life be like if you could achieve anything you set your mind on? Absolutely nothing would hold you back and you would be able to move ahead quickly and smoothly, achieving wealth, happiness, love, and everything else you desired along the way.

Life is not like that, of course. Life is a learning process, and we all experience ups and downs as we pass through it. We tend to blame others for the bad things that occur, but in actuality, we subconsciously attract everything that happens to us. In other words, it is usually our own thoughts that hold us back.

When we think positively, we attract positiveness into our lives, and this brings good things to us. Likewise, when we think thoughts of poverty, loss, and negativity, we attract those very things to us. Basically, we are magnets who attract to ourselves whatever it is we think about. Isn't it sad to think that we lead crippled lives, weighed down with negativity, when we could be leading lives of abundance, radiance, and happiness?

Wouldn't it be wonderful to have someone close by all the time who could help us attract these blessings to our lives—someone who could give us sound advice whenever we needed it; someone wise and intelligent, who always worked in our best interests; someone who was concerned only with our well-being; someone who wants to help us live a rich, successful, happy life?

The good news is that we do have such guides, even though most of us choose to ignore this fact. We can lead positive, rich, fulfilling lives because we are in touch with God through his angels and spirit guides. Knowledge of this can allow us to handle any crisis or catastrophe, because we have the certainty that God is looking after us and always has our well-being at heart.

These angels and spirit guides regularly give us advice, and sometimes we take it, but just as often choose to ignore it. As a child I was taught that angels looked after us. In prayers and hymns I heard about angels, and as a small child simply accepted the reality of them. As I grew older and began to question things, I found that even inside the established Church angels were considered almost an embarrassment. Consequently, I dismissed them as quaint relics from the past.

It took a major disaster in my life for me to realize that angels do exist and are there to protect and help us. In my middle twenties my business collapsed. I was married and my wife was expecting our first child. It could not have happened at a worse time. We had to sell our home and car and move to a small rented apartment. For a while I worked in a warehouse to make enough money to pay our bills.

This work was not very demanding and I had plenty of time to think about what had happened. It took me a long while to realize that much of our misfortune was of my own making. If I had made different decisions, the outcome would have been quite different and I would still have been running my own business instead of doing a menial job for someone else.

Once I accepted this, I also realized that all along I had been given advice by someone, but had chosen to ignore it. The still, quiet voice that we all hear, all day, every day, had consistently given me good advice, but I had not taken it. I did not know where that voice came from at that time. I probably called it my conscience or my inner mind. In fact, it was my guardian angel.

Like me, you have probably heeded this inner voice at times and ignored it at others. I always take notice of it now, as I know that my guardian angel has my best interests at heart. When I follow the advice of my guardian angel I cannot help doing the right things and taking the right actions. We all do things that we regret later. This happens much less frequently now that I pay attention to my guardian angel.

Why Communicate Through Angels and Guides?

You may wonder why we communicate with God through his intermediaries, rather than directly. In fact, throughout the Bible, God spoke to people more often through messengers than by direct contact. Here are some examples.

In the Old Testament, Lot spoke with two angels (Gen. 19: 1–3); an angel of the Lord saved Elijah from starving to death (1 Kings 19: 5–8); and Abraham heard from God in a dream (Gen. 20: 6). In the New Testament, the angel Gabriel came to Zacharias and told him that he and Elizabeth would have a son (Luke 1: 26–31); at Jesus' baptism "he saw the Spirit of God descending like a dove, and lighting upon him" (Matt. 3:16); and an angel told Mary Magdalene that Jesus had risen from the dead (Matt. 28: 5–7).

In other religions the same things apply. It was Gabriel, again, who communicated with Muhammad. The religion of Islam came about as a result of this encounter.

Throughout history, men and women have prayed to the Virgin Mary, Jesus, and the saints, as well as God, and expected an answer. In fact, every time we pray we are making a spirit contact. Consequently, when we communicate with our spirit guides or angels we are sending a message directly to God.

If we are able to communicate with the architect of the universe in this way, and receive solutions to our problems and difficulties, shouldn't we then be able to achieve anything we want? The answer is: we can. We should all be living lives of abundance!

Fortunately, by contacting our guides and angels we are much closer to the creative intelligence behind the universe than totally materialistic people are. We can receive help instantly. The Book of Isaiah says: "Before they call, I will answer; and while they are yet speaking, I will hear" (chapter 65, verse 24).

We all have a veritable army of spirit beings who are working all the time to help us achieve our goals and become successful. By recognizing them, communicating with them, and welcoming them into our lives we can make our lives much fuller and richer in every way. By working in tune with the spirit world we can literally achieve anything. Knowledge of this can do wonders for our confidence and self-esteem. The Bible says: "I can do all things through Christ which strengtheneth me" (Philippians 4:13).

If you have not yet made contact with your spirit guides and guardian angels, start practicing every day until you succeed. Your teachers and protectors are waiting patiently for you to welcome them into your life.

The Benefits of Working With Guides

We become better balanced, more rounded people when we develop spiritually. We believe that we are made up of physical, mental, emotional, and spiritual components, but it is very seldom that you find someone with all four areas equally balanced. It is common, for instance, to find people who spend their lives at the gym, toning their bodies and achieving the peak of physical fitness. But the chances are that they are not spending a quarter of their time or energy on the other three aspects.

When we develop the spiritual side, we often help the other areas as well. People who choose a spiritual path embark on a life of inner growth and learning, thus helping the mental side of their makeup. They also become more in tune with the world around them and find things that used to bother them in the past are now of no account. Consequently, they are also developing emotionally. When people develop spiritually, many tend to regard their own bodies as temples to be looked after. As a result, they pay more attention to physical fitness.

Look after all four areas in your own life and you will gradually find yourself transformed. Other people will comment on your serenity and inner glow. They may not realize exactly what you have been doing, but they will be aware of the changes within you. You will feel better in every way and will be aware that you can achieve anything you set your mind on.

Although it is true that you can achieve anything you wish, your progress will be faster and smoother if you involve your spirit guides at every step. When I look back over my own life, I realize that many, if not all, of the mistakes that I have made would have been avoided if I had consulted with my guides before acting.

It is a good habit to set aside some time every day to communicate with your guides. I try to do this twice a day. This gives me a ten-minute respite to relax and gain clarification and help.

A relative of mine was once offered a position in a company that was the main competitor to the corporation he worked for. It seemed like a good idea, as he felt that he was simply marking time where he was, and was not progressing as fast as he wanted. The new job offered considerably more money, and as he was supporting a wife and two young children on his salary, this was a major inducement.

My cousin regularly asks his spirit guides for advice. In his daily meditation session he asked them if it was a good idea for him to accept the offer. In his own mind he had already decided to accept, so he was surprised at the reply he received. In the still, quiet time that followed his question a message came into his mind suggesting that he stay where he was, as a new division was about to be opened up and he would be asked to manage it.

He had learned from experience to act on what his guides told him, and rejected the job offer. Everyone he had told about the job offer thought he was crazy, and he had several times when he wondered if he had made the right decision. However, a few months later he was in charge of the new division, with a much more exciting opportunity than the one offered by the competition. The promotion also meant that he was financially better off than if he had moved.

By asking his guides for advice in this way, my cousin used a hidden edge that most people ignore. We all receive hunches or intuitions from time to time. Sometimes we act on them, but they are also frequently ignored and forgotten. These hunches come on a haphazard basis. My cousin contacts his guides every day and talks with them in exactly the same way he talks with any living person. He has built up excellent communication with the spirit realms and uses this contact to better himself in every area of his life. Consequently, the messages he receives are not random, like the intuitions everyone has every now and again. His guides are helping and directing him all the way through life.

You can be helped in exactly the same way. Naturally, you will have doubts and fears until you start working with your guides on a daily basis. These will quickly fade away once you start making regular contact. Trust your spirit guides. Let them help you become everything that you are capable of being. Truly, you have unlimited potential. With the help of your angel guardians and spirit guides you can achieve anything.

Part One

Angel Guardians

1

Angels

What is an angel? Dictionaries say that angels are spiritual beings who attend to God. They are also messengers from God. Martin Luther wrote that "an angel is a spiritual creature created by God without a body, for the service of Christendom and of the Church."[1]

These definitions seem to indicate that angels are seen only by spiritual people, but this is not the case. People of all religions, and no religion, have seen angels. The definition is further clouded by the fact that angels can appear in different ways to different people. Some are able to see them, while others are simply aware of them. Most people become aware of them only when they listen to the small voice inside that is usually known as the conscience.

Even the people who see them view them in different ways. A friend of mine who had a life-changing experience when he saw an angel told me that it terrified him at first. "It was huge, at least ten feet tall, and looked just like a person, except for its glistening wings."

A week after being told that, a lady came up to me after a lecture and told me that when she saw an angel it was "a little cupid that I wanted to hold and cuddle."

Angels can change shape and form whenever they wish. Naturally, they can also change appearance depending on whereabouts in the world they are working. In Africa, for instance, angels are likely to appear African, and in the Far East they are Asian. A friend of mine who lived in Japan for many years told me of an angel he saw in his office who looked Japanese and was wearing a kimono.

If you see an angel it may not be a traditional one dressed in flowing white robes, with a golden halo, carrying a gleaming sword or playing a harp. An angel may even choose to appear as a particularly ordinary-looking person. There are many recorded instances of this.

An interesting example of this is the experience of a friend of mine who woke up one morning to find that it had snowed heavily overnight and her car wouldn't start. As she had to get her two young children to school, she called a cab. When it arrived, her young son insisted that she come with them. She dropped the children off at school and asked to be taken to the shopping mall. It was only then that she realized she might not have enough money. She was a single mother and a taxi ride was a rare luxury. Fortunately, she had enough money to pay the cab driver, but not enough to get back home again.

She sat on a bench inside the mall for half an hour wondering what to do. Eventually, she phoned the different taxi companies to see if she could negotiate a special price to get her back home. None of them were interested.

She made up her mind to walk home and went outside. Immediately, a cab pulled up alongside her and the driver called her by name.

"I'm your driver, lady," he said. He consulted a piece of paper and read off her address. "That where you're going?"

Surprised and bewildered, she got into the cab and was driven home. When she got there, she opened her purse and asked what the fare was.

"Have this one on me," the driver said.

"Thank you," she said, feeling more confused than ever. She got out of the cab and looked at her front door. She suddenly felt that her brief "thank you" was less than adequate and turned around to thank the taxi driver again. The taxi and the driver had completely disappeared. Apart from the parked cars the street was empty.

A less dramatic example happened to an acquaintance of mine who found herself in the downtown area of Los Angeles late at night without her car keys or money. She had left her office in a rush, leaving her purse behind. While debating what to do, she prayed for help. While she was still praying a man she had never seen before went up to the front entrance of the office building she worked in and unlocked the doors. They exchanged greetings as she ran inside and went up to her office. When she came back down again, the man had gone. Thc following day she made extensive inquiries at all the other corporations in the building, as she wanted to thank him. No one knew anything about the man, and she has never seen him since. Not surprisingly, she is convinced that he was an angel who came in response to her prayer.

These are good examples of the ways angels can come to our aid when we least expect it. They generally appear when we need help and then simply disappear once the work has been done.

The History of Angels

Angels have appeared in countless religious traditions. The earliest accounts of them date from the times of the ancient Assyrians and Babylonians.[2] The Babylonians believed that we all have our own individual guardian angels. They considered these angels to be supernatural beings who looked after our best interests, stayed with us when we were good, and temporarily left us when we did wrong. They also carried requests to and from the gods.

The Israelites carried this cosmology a step further. They believed in one God, but he was assisted by countless angels who acted as mediators. The belief in angels played an important part in Jewish thought and literature, particularly in nonbiblical writings.[3] Christianity then took angels on board, but the belief in the Holy Spirit placed limits on how far angelology could go. In fact, in the Bible, there is a warning not to worship angels (Col. 2:18).[4]

The angelic tradition can be found in virtually all, if not all, of the major religions, but became most popular in Christianity, Judaism, and Islam. This is not surprising when you consider that Judaism and Christianity both share the Old Testament, and Islam was greatly influenced by the Old Testament also. The Jewish Diaspora was also strongly influenced by the Zoroastrian cosmology of angels, which dates back to at least the seventh century B.C.

Angels are mentioned some 300 times in the Bible.[5] One good example was when God sent an angel to help Daniel when he was in the lions' den. The angel came and shut the mouths of the hungry lions (Dan. 16:22). Another example is when God sent Saint Paul an angel to tell him that he would survive a shipwreck (Acts 27: 21–26).

In the Book of Job (38:7) there are indications that angels were enjoying life before the creation of the material world. Once the world was created angels were given the task of looking after and protecting people. In the Psalms (91:11–12) we are told:

> *For he shall give his angels charge over thee, to keep thee in all thy ways. They shall bear thee up in their hands, lest thou dash thy foot against a stone.*

A much more vivid example occurred in the Garden of Gethsemane when Jesus prayed (Luke 22:42–43), knowing that ahead of him was his crucifixion.

> *Father, if thou be willing, remove this cup from me: nevertheless not my will, but thine, be done. And there appeared an angel unto him from heaven, strengthening him.*

Angels also have the vitally important role of being messengers of God. Obviously, they have an important relationship with God, but are never able to witness the glory of God. With just one known exception angels have never been human. (The prophet Enoch, author of the Book of Enoch, was taken to heaven by the archangel Michael and God transformed him into an angel.) Angels can disguise themselves and appear in human form when they wish, but they are not the souls of people who have died. They are immortal, ageless, sexless (Matt. 22:30), and have the ability to make themselves visible or invisible. No one knows how many angels there are. In the Catholic Church it is believed that at birth everyone is given at least one guardian angel. The ancient Jewish teachings claim that every Jew has 11,000 guardian angels![6]

The number seven has always been considered to have special spiritual significance. The ancient Essenes were a Jewish sect who date back at least four thousand years. One of their beliefs was in a Tree of Life with seven branches reaching toward heaven and seven roots keeping it solidly rooted to the earth. These branches and roots were related to the seven mornings and evenings of the week, and to seven angels. The seven archangels of Christianity are derived from these. However, most knowledge of angels does not come from the Bible but from Pseudo-Dionysius, whose hierarchy of angels we will discuss in the next chapter.

Angels have also been recognized for thousands of years in India, and the Sanskrit literature contains numerous mentions of angels.[7] The Bhagavad Gita advises people to give daily offerings to angels.[8] Even today, orthodox Hindus conduct different rites and ceremonies for angels, as they believe that their well-being and prosperity depends on how well regarded they are by the angels.

The archangel Gabriel appeared before Muhammad and this led to the creation of Islam. Likewise, the appearance of the angel Moroni before Joseph Smith on September 21, 1823, led to the creation of the Church of Jesus Christ of Latter-Day Saints.

Joan of Arc was a farm girl who became the leader of the French army that forced the English out of her country during the Hundred Years' War after hearing angels' voices. Apparently she saw angels several times a week. Joan of Arc said: "I saw them (angels) with my bodily eyes as clearly as I see you. And when they departed I used to weep and wish that they would take me with them."[9]

Joan of Arc was also gifted with telepathic, clairvoyant, and precognitive abilities. For instance, she was able to tell the king the words of a prayer that he had composed in his head. She was able to "see" clairvoyantly a sword that was hidden behind the altar of a church. She also showed people the place on her body where she was going to be wounded by an arrow in the imminent battle for Orleans. A Flemish diplomat wrote down her premonition before the battle, and it proved to be correct in every detail.[10]

The concept of a personal guardian angel took a large step forward in about 150 C.E. when Hermas wrote down his experiences with his personal angel-shepherd. His book, *Shepherd of Hermas*, became extremely popular, as it encouraged people to consider angels their own personal shepherds of God.[11]

In the thirteenth century, Thomas Aquinas (1225–1274), known as the "Angelic Doctor" because of his amazing intellect, wrote eighteen large books, creating a virtual encyclopedia of religious thought. His most famous book, *Summa Theologiae*, contains fifteen of his lectures on angels, which he originally presented in just one week. Many of Aquinas' ideas were not accepted at the time, but the Roman Catholic reformers at the Council of Trent (1545–1563) used his works in composing their decrees, giving Aquinas a prominence in the Roman Catholic church that has lasted to the present day. In 1879, the pope declared that Aquinas' theology was "eternally valid."

For some two hundred years people considered angels to be part of an obsolete, outmoded cosmology. However, today they are making a comeback. Psychologists take the subject seriously. Carl Jung believed implicitly in angels and described them as "soulless beings who represent nothing but the thoughts and intuitions of their Lord."[12] As well, many hundreds of thousands, if not millions, of people around the world can attest to having seen angels. In most cases, this experience becomes one of the most treasured memories of a whole lifetime.

Angel Work

Angels usually act as messengers between heaven and earth, though they are also considered to be guides, protectors and nurturers. In fact, the word angel comes from the Greek word angelos, which is derived from the Hebrew word *mal'akh*, meaning "messenger."

Angels normally work with us on a one-to-one basis, and these are usually our guardian angels. However, there have also been recorded instances where large numbers of angels were seen. Probably the most famous example of this is when an angel of the Lord appeared to the shepherds to tell them about the birth of Jesus. After he had told them his message he was suddenly surrounded by a multitude of angels (Luke 2:13). A modern example is the appearance of a "whole company of angels" on a hillside at Lee Abbey in North Devon in 1952.[13]

There are many accounts of groups of angels assisting the British forces during World War I. The first appearance of angels was in 1915, and their assistance continued until the end of the war. They are usually known as the "Angels of Mons" because this is where they were first seen.

In July 1918, the German forces saw a brigade of cavalry approaching them. The men were not dressed in khaki, but wore white uniforms and rode white horses. The Germans repeatedly fired at this brigade, but the soldiers kept on moving towards them with no apparent casualties. Even the machine guns made no impression. The leader of the brigade rode a few paces ahead of the others. His hair looked like spun gold and appeared almost like an aura around his head. By his side was a huge sword, but his hands rested lightly on his stallion's reins. Suddenly, as one, the German soldiers turned and ran, terrified of this strange White Cavalry.[14]

These examples show that angels are still active in the world today. However, many people dismiss the subject, considering angels the subject of myths and fairy tales. Perhaps this is why people who have seen angels usually keep quiet about it. Even if you have not seen an angel yourself, I am sure that you know someone who has. However, this person may well be keeping it a secret, because he or she does not want to risk being ridiculed.

In past centuries, people would discuss angels freely. Nowadays, even members of the clergy are often reluctant to discuss the subject. This is surprising when one considers that the Catholic Church celebrates Saint Michael and All Angels every year on September 29. The Roman Catholic Church is even more specific and celebrates the feast of Saints Michael, Gabriel, and Raphael, all archangels, on this day.

Angels can appear at any time and anywhere. In the Epistle to the Hebrews (13:2), Saint Paul says: "Be not forgetful to entertain strangers; for thereby some have entertained angels unawares."

Angels probably exist as images and need our input to be brought to life. Carl Jung believed in universal images that were common to everyone. Guardian angels are certainly universal images to humankind as a whole. Accepting their existence allows us to open our souls and allow them into our lives.

Believing in spirit guides and angels allows us to make contact with our higher selves, which releases our intuition and creativity, and makes angels real. G. Don Gilmore, a minister and writer in Spokane, Washington, describes angels as "forms, images or expressions through which the essences and energy forces of God can be transmitted."[15]

In the past, groups of people would manifest angels, but this is done rarely now.[16] However, it is possible to do this individually, and we will be doing that later in this book to enable you to locate your own personal guardian angel.

The Celestial Hierarchy

There is a celestial hierarchy, or holy order, of angels which was first written down by Pseudo-Dionysius the Areopagite in the fifth century.[17] Pseudo-Dionysius studied the Book of Enoch and many other Jewish and Christian writings in an attempt to clarify the different rankings of the angels. He finally came up with nine choirs of angels, which are arranged into three groups or triads.

First Triad	**Second Triad**
1. Seraphim.	4. Dominions.
2. Cherubim.	5. Virtues.
3. Thrones.	6. Powers.

Third Triad

7. Principalities.
8. Archangels.
9. Angels.[18]

The choirs in the first triad are the angels who are always in the presence of God. They are known as "God's faithful angels." According to Saint Thomas, the angels of the first triad never come down to earth.

The seraphim are the angels closest to God, and their main task is to encircle the throne of God while saying the Kadosh, a famous Hebrew prayer that is still used today ("Holy, holy, holy"). According to Enoch there are four seraphim, "corresponding to the four winds of the world."

The seraphim are beings of perfect light who shine so brilliantly that few humans could ever look at them. The few prophets who have seen them describe them as "flaming angels." Pseudo-Dionysius said that the word *seraphim* means both "those that warm" and "those that burn." They are the angels of love, but also the angels of light and fire.

The cherubim are the guardians of the stars and the path to the Tree of Life. The word *cherubim* means "those who pray," "those who intercede," and "fullness of knowledge."

They are ready to provide us with protection and knowledge when we are ready to receive it. The prophet Ezekiel, one of the few people to have seen the cherubim, described them as having four faces and four wings (Ezek. 1:6). Many people see them as half human and half beast. This might be because Ezekiel described the head of an angel of the cherubim as having the face of a man in the front, a lion on the right, an ox on the left, and an eagle at the back (Ezek. 1:10). The cherubim are the first angels mentioned in the Old Testament (Gen. 3:22).

The Thrones or Wheels (sometimes known as Ophanim) act as God's transportation. Their task is the transfer of positive energy. They focus this energy to reveal injustices and send healing energy to people who need it. Interestingly enough, it is believed that they do not send this energy to us directly, but usually through our personal guardian angels.[19]

The angels of the Second Triad are the organizing and ministering angels. They are more concerned with the universe than individuals, but have been known to assist on earth when required.

The Dominions make sure that every angel is fully utilized. They carry out the orders given by the angels of the First Triad and carry orbs and scepters as symbols of their authority. The Virtues provide strength, courage, and motivation. They provide spiritual energy when needed and enable people to achieve much more than they think they can. The Powers protect heaven and are considered to be warrior angels. They also help us decide between right and wrong, and ensure that the laws of the universe stay in operation.

The angels of the Third Triad are the ones who are most involved with life on earth.

The Principalities have the task of looking after continents, nations, cities, and any other large groups. They constantly transfer information to and from heaven. They also have the task of ensuring that our world leaders receive good advice and act wisely.

The archangels are God's most important messengers. In Islam four archangels are recognized, but the Christian tradition considers seven angels to be archangels. Each archangel has a name and special duties to perform.

The angels are assigned to individuals and are often referred to as guardian angels. They are present at our birth, stay with us throughout life, and help us at the end of this incarnation. The guardian angels work with all the other angels in the nine choirs. When we need help, our guardian angels can obtain it from any other angel or from God.

In the seventeenth century John Milton added to angelic lore with his twelve-volume epic poem *Paradise Lost*. One hundred years later, Emanuel Swedenborg, a leading scientist of the day, went into trances that sometimes lasted for days. In these trances he visited the spirit world, which he recorded in great detail.[20]

The Archangels

Anyone who attended Sunday school as a child will know the names of at least some of the archangels. In the second century B.C.E. Enoch described his visit to the heavens. This was the first time all seven archangels were named. The Old Testament names Michael and Gabriel. However, the only angel who is specifically called an archangel in the Bible is Michael (Jude 9). The seven angels who stand before God in the Book of Revelation are usually considered to be the seven archangels. (Rev. 15–17) The names of these seven angels are: Michael, Gabriel, Raphael, Uriel, Raguel, Sariel, and Remiel. The first four of these (known as the "Four Angels of the Presence") are also the archangels of Islam. You will notice that the name of each archangel ends with *el*. This means "shining being."

Angels are neither male nor female. Consequently, for example, if the angel Michael visits you, it will not necessarily be as a masculine-looking angel. Michael could appear in any shape or form, depending on the situation and circumstances.

Michael

Michael is by far the best known of the archangels. In the Roman Catholic Church he is also referred to as Saint Michael. Catholics pray to Saint Michael the archangel to protect them from evil. He is also regarded as the protector of the Catholic Church. The name Michael means "one who is like God." Michael is believed to be the archangel closest to God. He has always been considered the special friend and defender of the Jewish people. It is believed that Michael will appear whenever the world is in great danger.

Rudolf Steiner (1861–1925), the Austrian philosopher who founded the Anthroposophical Society, believed that Michael had been promoted from archangel and become an archai, which allowed him to put all his efforts into helping humanity as a whole.[21]

Michael is credited with stopping Abraham from sacrificing his son Isaac (Gen. 22:10). He also appeared to Moses in the burning bush (Exod. 3:2) and rescued Daniel from the lion's den (Dan. 6:22). He is also believed to have been seen by Joan of Arc.

The Feast of Michaelmas dates from the fifth century. It became extremely important during the Middle Ages because Michael is the patron saint of knights. Today, the Anglicans and Catholics celebrate Saint Michael on September 29. He is honored on November 8 in the Greek, Armenian, Russian, and Coptic churches.

Represents: Love.
Element: Fire.
Direction: South.
Season: Autumn.
Color: Red.
Zodiac Signs: Aries, Leo, and Sagittarius.

Gabriel

Gabriel sits on the left-hand side of God and is the second most important archangel. Although angels are considered to be neither male nor female, Gabriel is usually pictured as female, even though she has appeared in masculine form at different times. The name Gabriel means "God is my strength." Gabriel has traditionally been considered God's envoy to humankind.

Gabriel has a strong connection with pregnancy and birth, for a number of reasons. It was Gabriel who visited Zacharias and told him that Elizabeth, his wife, would give birth to John the Baptist (Luke 1:11–20). Gabriel also visited Mary and told her that she would give birth to Jesus (Luke 1:26–35). In the Catholic Church the "Hail Mary" is believed to be the greeting that Gabriel used when visiting Mary.[22] In Catholic tradition Gabriel also told the shepherds of Jesus' birth.[23] The Catholic Church celebrates the Feast of Saint Gabriel on March 24. Gabriel also told Daniel about the coming of the Messiah (Dan. 9:21–27).

It was Gabriel who went to Mount Hira and told Muhammad that he was a prophet, a god. Islam began at that moment. Gabriel is known as Gibrail to the Muslims, who also believe that he dictated the Koran.[24]

In 1862, in New Zealand, Gabriel appeared before the Maori prophet Te Ua Haumene and gave him the necessary strength to free himself from the ropes that had been used to confine him. Te Ua later said that Gabriel, Michael, and "an innumerable host of ministering spirits" had appeared around him.[25]

Like all angels, Gabriel can appear in any form. When Gabriel appeared to Muhammad his body blotted out half of the sky, which resounded to the sound of his wings. However, the Sufi Ruzbehan Baqli saw him in quite a different way:

> *In the first rank I saw Gabriel, like a maiden, or like the moon amongst the stars. His hair was like a woman's, falling in long tresses. He wore a red robe embroidered in green...He is the most beautiful of Angels...His face is like a red rose.*[26]

Represents: Overcoming doubt and fear.
Element: Water.
Direction: West.
Season: Winter.
Color: Emerald.
Zodiac Signs: Cancer, Scorpio, and Pisces.

Raphael

Raphael is the third most important archangel. The name Raphael means "shining one who heals." Raphael is not mentioned by name in the Bible but appears in the apocryphal Old Testament Book of Tobit. He is believed to heal the wounds of martyrs and protect travelers. The Catholic Church used to celebrate Saint Raphael on October 24, but with the tidying-up of the liturgical calendar he is now usually celebrated on September 29, which is called "Saint Michael and All Angels."

Represents:	Healing.
Element:	Air.
Direction:	East.
Season:	Spring.
Color:	Blue.
Zodiac Signs:	Gemini, Libra, and Aquarius.

Uriel

Uriel is the last of the Four Angels of the Presence. The name Uriel means "Fire of God." Uriel is often known as the Angel of Repentance and meets the souls of sinners as they arrive in heaven. Uriel is highly versatile. He is also the Angel of Music, and is believed to have been sent by God to warn Noah of the impending flood. In the Jewish tradition, he is believed to have given the Kabbalah to the Jews.

Represents:	Clear thinking.
Element:	Earth.
Direction:	North.
Season:	Summer.
Color:	White.
Zodiac Signs:	Taurus, Virgo, and Capricorn.

Raguel

The name Raguel means "Friend of God." Raguel is the angel who took Enoch to heaven. Enoch said that he makes sure the other angels maintain high standards of behavior.

Sariel

We know about Sariel from the Book of Enoch. He is the angel responsible for disciplining the angels who misbehave. In some traditions it is believed that he was the angel who taught Moses.

Remiel

Remiel is known as the Angel of Hope. The name Remiel means "God raises up," which gives a clue as to his main task—leading souls to heaven.

Metatron

In the Kabbalah the most important angel is Metatron, whose name means "closest to the throne." Metatron is not an archangel, but is often referred to as King of the Angels. He lives up to this title by being the tallest and most imposing angel of all. He is described as being between eight and thirteen feet tall, with thirty-six wings and numerous eyes that allow him to watch over the entire world.

Metatron is the only human being who became an angel. Enoch was borne to heaven, where God had Michael anoint him with oil, transformed him into an angel, and renamed him Metatron.

The Angel of the Lord

There is some evidence to indicate that Jesus Christ visited earth as an angel before his incarnation. The Book of Genesis tells how Hagar ran away from Sarai, her mistress, after becoming pregnant. The angel of the Lord found her by a fountain of water in the wilderness. The angel told her: "Behold, thou art with child, and shalt bear a son, and shalt call his name Ishmael (Gen. 16:11). In verse 13 "she called the name of the Lord that spake unto her, Thou God seest me." Obviously, in this account, the angel of the Lord and God are one and the same.

The same situation occurs in the Book of Exodus when an angel appeared to Moses in the burning bush. Chapter 3, verses 2 to 4 read:

> *And the angel of the Lord appeared unto him in a flame of fire out of the midst of a bush: and he looked, and, behold, the bush burned with fire, and the bush was not consumed.*
>
> *And Moses said, I will now turn aside, and see this great sight, why the bush is not burnt.*
>
> *And when the Lord saw that he turned aside to see, God called unto him out of the midst of the bush, and said, Moses, Moses. And he said, Here am I.*

Again the angel of the Lord and God are one and the same. Consequently, it appears that the angel of the Lord, at least in the Old Testament, is a visible appearance of Jesus Christ.

The Queen of Angels

On the morning of July 18, 1830, Catherine Laboure, a member of the Sisters of Charity, woke to the sight of a beautiful angel. "Go to the chapel quickly," the angel told her. Catherine hastened to obey and found herself in the presence of the Virgin Mary. She told Catherine that she was the blessed mother of all children and was known as the Queen of Angels.

For many months after this visitation, Catherine spent her time in contemplation and prayer. She returned to the chapel every morning hoping to see the Queen of Angels again.

One morning the Queen appeared, standing upon a globe surrounded by a pure light, and clothed by the sun. She opened her hands and fiery rays of light leapt from the rings she wore on each finger, igniting the globe. The Queen told Catherine that the globe represented the earth and the fiery rays symbolized the help she is able to give children who ask for it. Sadly, the rings that did not emit rays of light symbolized children who forgot to ask for help.

The Queen of Angels then told Catherine that it was the will of God that a medal of protection be made depicting the scene to represent God's unconditional love and to grant protection to anyone who carries it.

Millions of copies of this medal have been made and worn since Catherine's vision. It is known as "The Miraculous Medal."[27] Catherine was later beatified and canonized as Saint Catherine Laboure.

The Queen of Angels became another name for the Virgin Mary. She is also sometimes referred to as the Angel of Peace. There have been numerous recorded apparitions of Mary over the last 2,000 years, and it is interesting to note that these appearances have increased in the nineteenth and twentieth centuries.

Probably the most momentous of these visitations occurred in Lourdes, France. From February 11 to July 16, 1858, the Virgin Mary appeared numerous times to Bernadette Soubirous, a fourteen-year-old peasant girl, in the Massabielle grotto. This rocky grotto on the left side of the stream quickly became a shrine and today some three million people a year visit Lourdes. A basilica was built above the grotto in 1876, but could not accommodate the ever-increasing number of pilgrims. In 1958 a huge underground church that can seat 20,000 people was built.[28]

An interesting test of the healing waters from Lourdes was conducted at the University of Naples. Samples of the Lourdes water and ordinary tap water were contaminated with poisonous germs and then injected into guinea pigs. The animals that had been injected with ordinary water died, but the ones injected with Lourdes water were not affected.[29]

The Queen of Angels also made herself visible at Fatima, Portugal. On May 13, 1917, a lady who identified herself as the Lady of the Rosary appeared before three shepherd children, Lucia dos Santos and her cousins Francisco and Jacinta Marto. She appeared again each month until October. On October 13 a crowd of some

70,000 people witnessed a "miraculous solar phenomenon" immediately after the Lady of the Rosary appeared to the children. On October 13, 1930, the Bishop of Leiria finally accepted that the visitations were from the Virgin Mary, and papal indulgences for pilgrims were granted. However, the first national pilgrimage to Fatima took place in 1927. On May 13, 1967, one million people gathered at Fatima to hear Pope Paul VI say Mass on the fiftieth anniversary of the first vision. Numerous healings have been recorded at Fatima, though these are not generally publicized.[30]

You can call on the Queen of Angels for assistance whenever you need help with, or for, young children.

The Fallen Angels

No book on angels would be complete without at least some reference to the fallen angels.

When God created the angels the most beautiful of all was Lucifer, the light-bearer. Unfortunately, the archangel Lucifer rebelled against God's authority. The Book of the Prophet Ezekiel says: "Thou wast perfect in thy ways from the day that thou wast created, till iniquity was found in thee" (Ezek. 28:15). The Book of Isaiah describes the sins that Lucifer committed:

> *For thou hast said in thine heart, I will ascend into heaven, I will exalt my throne above the stars of God: I will sit also upon the mount of the congregation, in the*

> *sides of the north: I will ascend above the heights of the clouds; I will be like the most High* (Isa. 14: 13–14).

Not surprisingly, Lucifer was thrown out of heaven and into hell. Many other angels went with him. In *Paradise Lost*, Milton gives a vivid account of the fall:

> *Him the Almighty Power*
> *Hurled headlong flaming from the ethereal sky,*
> *With hideous ruin and combustion, down*
> *To bottomless perdition; there to dwell*
> *In adamantine chains and penal fire,*
> *Who durst defy the Omnipotent to arms.*[31]

This "fall" has been a popular theme for writers and artists, but remains an unresolved mystery. Why would a merciful, loving God allow his enemy to fill his creation, the world, with hate, suffering, and evil?

There is a pre-Christian tradition that sheds light on this. In these ancient Eastern writings, Lucifer is referred to as one of the seven angels of the solar system. He was guardian of Venus, which was considered to be the holiest of all planets.

One day, God asked his leading angels for a volunteer to go down to earth to help humankind. The task was to lead people through different temptations to strengthen their faith and spirituality. Lucifer volunteered, and over a period of time, became regarded as the devil. Many stories were told about him, and the storytellers gradually forgot that Lucifer was sent down by God to test humankind. Instead, he became regarded as a force for evil.

Lucifer represents the dark side of life and is necessary, because without dark there would not be any light. Without evil, there would not be any good. These opposites, like yin and yang, create a perfect whole.[32]

2

Your Guardian Angel

Whether or not you are presently aware of it, you have your own personal guardian angel. This fact has proven controversial to theologians throughout history. If each of us has a guardian angel, obviously the population of heaven must be much greater than that of earth. In the Bible it is recorded that a thousand thousands served God, and ten thousand times ten thousand stood before him (Dan. 7:10). The population of the world is steadily increasing, but the number of angels is fixed, and does not increase or decrease.

In the Psalms it is recorded that "He will give his angels charge of you, to guard you in all your ways" (Psalms 91:11). This is a clear message that we each have been given a special angel to look after us.

Jesus also referred to the guardian angels of children when he said that their angels always behold the face of his Father (Matt. 18:10).

In 379 C.E. Saint Basil wrote that everyone who believes in God has a guardian angel. The medieval theologian, Thomas Aquinas, said that everyone is given a guardian angel at birth, and this angel "continually lights, guards, rules and guides."[1]

There are many stories about Saint Patrick, the patron saint of Ireland, and his guardian angel, Victoricus, who frequently appeared to him in visions and dreams. Saint Patrick came from a wealthy family in Roman Britain, but was kidnapped and became a slave in Ireland. Saint Patrick's first experience with angels came when he heard an angelic voice that gave him detailed plans on how to escape to the south of Ireland where a ship was waiting to take him away.[2] This must have been his guardian angel.

In France, a common greeting when two farmers met each other was, "Good day to you and your companion." The companion would be the farmer's guardian angel.

For hundreds of years Catholic children have been taught a prayer that also reaffirms belief in guardian angels:

Angel of God who are my guardian,
enlighten, watch over, support and rule me,
who was entrusted to you by the heavenly piety.
Amen.

Padre Pio was a Catholic priest who experienced stigmata. This means that the signs of Christ's crucifixion appeared on his hands and feet. He spent his entire life in intimate contact with his guardian angel. Fortunately, he wrote down many of his experiences with angels, and some of these were used by Father Alessio Parente when he wrote *Send Me Your Guardian Angels, Padre Pio*. In this biography Father Parente wrote: "Padre Pio's spiritual guidance of souls was mostly done through the help and direction of his Guardian Angel."[3] Padre Pio's guardian angel was also able to translate the many letters he received from all over the world, and enable him to reply to the letter-writers in their own language. The Roman Catholic Church is currently considering Padre Pio for beatification.

Pope Pius XI (1857–1939) is reported as telling a group of people that he prayed to his guardian angel every morning and night. If he was going to speak to someone who might disagree with his views, he would ask his guardian angel to speak to the other person's guardian angel first. The two guardian angels would agree quickly, allowing the contact between the Pope and his visitor to proceed smoothly and easily.[4] A later pope, John XXIII (1881–1963), was also a strong believer in guardian angels and frequently mentioned them in his radio talks. Regularly, these talks encouraged parents to teach their children that they were never alone, but had guardian angels looking after them.[5]

In 1968, Pope Paul VI (1897–1978) sanctioned the establishment of the Opus Sanctorum Angelorum ("the Work of the Holy Angels"). This organization, known as "Opus" for short, has a number of aims, including encouraging a belief in guardian angels. The initiates of this organization progress through three stages.

The first stage lasts for one year. During this time the initiates promise God that they will love their guardian angels and will act on their wishes. They also learn the names of their own personal guardian angels. During the second stage the initiates take part in a candlelit ceremony and promise to become like angels and to venerate angels. The final stage includes a ceremony of consecration to the entire angelic hierarchy.

The idea of a wise, protective spirit looking after our well-being has been an extremely comforting thought for people of all faiths, and none, for thousands of years.

Origen (c. A.D. 185–253), one of the early fathers of the Christian Church, believed that we each have two guardian angels, one good and the other evil. This is related to the ancient Greek belief in daimones, who acted as intermediaries between earth and heaven. The good daimone encouraged you to stay on the right path, while the bad one tempted you into evil.

Some authorities claim that our guardian angels are assigned to us either at conception or birth. I am inclined to believe that birth would be the logical time for the guardian angel to appear. All the same, this does not stop me from preferring the ancient tradition that says the guardian angel appears when the baby first laughs.

Experiences of Angels

Once the guardian angel has arrived, it stays with us throughout our lives and helps us go through the transition of death. Many near-death experiences from all over the world confirm this hypothesis.

A friend of mine had a near-death experience while undergoing an operation to remove his tonsils.

"I found myself floating over the operating table, looking down on the people who were working on my body. It was strange, as I experienced no emotion, but was aware of absolutely everything.

"At the same time I was aware of an incredible light. It started faintly, but rapidly grew until I was completely enfolded in it, and it felt fantastic. I cannot begin to describe the power or intensity of this light. It was the most beautiful thing I have ever seen. It should have dazzled me, it was so intense, but it didn't, probably because it was so pure. And it was filled with love. I felt totally surrounded by love. It wasn't just a light, either. It was a being, a being of light.

"I knew I was dying, but I was happy. I did not want to come back. I have a good life, but this feeling was so perfect, so exhilarating, that I wanted to stay there forever. I seemed to feel, rather than hear, a voice telling me, 'not yet, not yet,' and I was suddenly back inside my body. However, I must tell you that since that time I have had no fear of death."

My friend's experience with this light is similar to many other accounts.[6] Many of these people have referred to this light as their guardian angel. Some have even recognized it from childhood experiences and have regretted the long period of time when they ignored their guardian angels' offers of help and protection.

Many young children are also aware of their angel guardians. They often call these invisible friends by name, and take them everywhere with them. Some years ago I sat down in a friend's car and was immediately confronted by the owner's young daughter, who admonished me for sitting on her friend. Naturally, I made amends as much as I could by picking up the imaginary friend, cuddling it, apologizing, and then holding it on my knee for the duration of the ride.

A small boy was trapped under the ruins of an earthquake in Taormina, Sicily, for many days. His rescuers could not believe that he had survived so long, but the boy declared that a lady in "shining white garments" had brought him food every day.[7]

Sadly, these imaginary friends are usually educated out of us. Some find them again late in life. Paola Giovetti relates an experience when an old lady suddenly said, "He's back again!" When asked to explain, she said that when she was a small girl "he" was always beside her, but then she completely forgot about him. This lady died the next day, happy in the knowledge that "he" would be waiting for her.[8]

Your guardian angel knows everything about you and is willing to help you in any way at all to make your life as rich and fulfilling as possible. You can have no secrets from your guardian angel. If you are envious of someone, your guardian angel will know. If you are tempted to be dishonest, your special angel will know. You may hear a small inner voice talking to you, telling you not to do it. You may call this your conscience. I have learned to call it my guardian angel.

Some years ago I gave a series of lectures at a maximum security prison. I was interested to hear from several of the inmates that just a few seconds had made all the difference to them being locked up now, rather than enjoying freedom on the outside. They had all had a few seconds when a small inner voice told them not to do whatever it was they were planning. If they had listened to their inner voice they would still be enjoying life outside. However, they chose to ignore the advice of their guardian angel and now had plenty of time to reflect on the difference that just a few seconds can make. In many ways they reminded me of the saying, "The devil made me do it."

Incidentally, one of the inmates had come to know his guardian angel after being imprisoned. He had badly beaten and almost killed a neighbor after a domestic dispute.

"I had a history of violence," he told me. "My dad used to beat me up all the time, so I beat up other kids, smaller kids. When I grew up I joined a gang and was in fights all the time. When I got married I tried to put it all behind me. Every time I had violent thoughts, I bottled them all up. One day I just exploded." He shook his head at the memory. "It was awful being totally out of control, and it cost me everything." At the time I spoke to him his wife was obtaining a divorce. "Anyway, just two days after arriving here I woke up one morning and there was this huge angel standing beside my bed. I wanted to scream, I was so terrified, but everything scared me those first few days, and I didn't want to attract attention to myself. He was dressed in white robes and everything seemed to gleam. The white was not ordinary white. It was somehow pure and perfect, and once I got used to him, my heart stopped racing.

"'What do you want?' I asked. The angel said nothing, but just looked at me. The compassion and understanding in his eyes made me cry. I felt so ashamed of myself and what I'd done. While I was crying, he rested his hand on my shoulder and I felt a tingle go through my whole body. It was like a small electric shock, but it was a good feeling. I suddenly felt happier than I'd been in months—years, probably. And then he just disappeared.

"My cellmate slept through the whole thing. I didn't tell him. I didn't tell anyone, but I waited and waited for him to come back again. I don't mind waiting. I've got time to burn.

"It took ages for him to come back. Maybe three months. Anyway, I woke up one morning and there he was again. I asked him where he'd been and he said he was waiting for me to call him. 'Why would I call you?' I asked.

'You can call me whenever you need me,' he said. Then he was gone.

"'Come back!' I called out, and then I heard this voice inside me saying, 'Be at peace. I'm with you all the time.' And he is. I know he's there. I hardly ever see him, but he's definitely there."

This formerly violent man is now a model prisoner. I am confident that with the help of his guardian angel he will be a good citizen once he is released from prison. He now knows that he has to listen to that still, quiet voice inside.

This man met his guardian angel when he was at the lowest point of his whole life. Guardian angels frequently appear when everything seems hopeless.

Debra, a woman I met after one of my lectures, told me that her guardian angel appeared to her when her son committed suicide. "Without my guardian angel I would have killed myself," she said. "Life didn't seem worth living anymore. It took time, of course, but with the help of my angel I've got my life back together again, and I'm very happy."

The prisoner I spoke to was terrified when he first saw an angel. This is a common occurrence. In fact, in the Bible, almost every angelic appearance begins with the angel saying, "Fear not!"

Children are often able to see their guardian angels. Sadly, they tend to lose this ability as they grow. Often the actions of adults who make fun of their "imaginary friends" cause this to happen.

I had an interesting experience some years ago with a boy who had an extremely protective guardian angel. His mother brought him to me in my work as a hypnotherapist because he was an elective mute. This means that he was able to talk, but chose not to, unless he was with people he felt totally secure with. Naturally, this situation was causing a great deal of distress and worry to his parents. Tony (not his real name) had started life as a normal child, but became an elective mute at the age of five. He had never spoken with the teachers or other children at school, and had no friends. Surprisingly, he was good at team sports, even though he never uttered a word while playing. He was also an A student.

Tony was a good hypnotic subject and on his first session I gave suggestions that he would be comfortable talking with me. When he opened his eyes he started talking and did not stop for twenty minutes. His mother, sitting outside in the waiting room, could hardly believe it as she heard the stream of conversation through the door. She had told me that he was always like this when he returned home from school each day.

On the second visit I tried to take him back to whatever situation caused him to become mute. I did not succeed in this, on that occasion, but halfway through the session he suddenly said, "My angel's with me."

"That's good," I replied. "Does your angel have a name?"

"Of course," he retorted. "His name's Dana."

"Does he help you?"

"'Course he does. He's my friend."

When he opened his eyes again I asked Tony to tell me about his angel. Tony obviously felt secure in my company and he told me about Dana in great detail.

Dana was a tall angel with beautiful white wings. He usually wore dazzling white robes, but sometimes wore a red outfit that looked something like pajamas. Tony and he talked all the time to each other, but did not need to speak out loud. Dana helped him in class by answering the questions that Tony did not know. Dana also helped Tony play games by telling him what to do. Dana had even saved Tony's life by holding him back when he would have stepped off the pavement into the path of a passing truck.

Tony told me all of this in a matter-of-fact tone. After several minutes, he asked, "Do you believe me?"

"Of course," I replied. "We all have a guardian angel."

Tony was surprised. "Everyone? Even Mum and Dad?"

"Everyone."

"Why don't people talk about them then?"

"Some people do," I said. "You've told me all about Dana."

"But you're the first person I've told."

"Dana doesn't mind you talking to other people," I said. "You can still talk to Dana in your head whenever you want. He will always be there to help you. But I'm sure he wouldn't want you to talk only to him. Why don't you ask him if he minds you talking to other people?"

Tony nodded his head and was silent for half a minute.

"He says I can talk to other people, but mustn't tell them about him. He wants it to be a secret."

"That's a good idea," I said.

Three days later Tony's mother phoned me to say that Tony had started speaking at school. In fact, he was talking nonstop, as all the children were lining up to have a conversation with him.

Tony had always been aware of his guardian angel. Many people find their angels later on in life.

Elizabeth, a shy college student, found it hard to tell her story, as she had never told it to anyone before.

"I was playing netball," she said. "It was the high school championships and I was the goal shooter. I was nervous and was missing even the easy shots. I was scared in case I let my team down. I'm not a Christian, but I said, 'Please, God, help me.' Next time I looked at the goal there was a little angel sitting on it. I couldn't believe my eyes. I wasn't scared 'cause the angel looked so perfect and cute. It was definitely a girl angel, so petite and feminine. I wanted to pick her up and cuddle her. I couldn't believe that no one else could see her. Anyway, next time I shot a goal my angel helped it go in. And she did it again and again. We won by miles and I was the hero of the day.

"Ever since then my guardian angel has been around to help me whenever I need it. Of course, I know she was there before, but I never realized it." Elizabeth smiled and shook her head. "All those wasted years!"

Bob met his guardian angel on his wedding day. "Terry—he's my best man—and I arrived really early at the church. I didn't want to go in too soon, so we parked the car and wandered around the cemetery beside the church. It was a beautiful day, the start of spring, and the trees looked gorgeous and the birds were singing—a magic day.

"'What a great day to get married on,' I said to Terry. He laughed and there right beside him was an angel. I pointed at it and said, 'Look at that!' but Terry couldn't see it. He laughed at me and I made him promise not to tell anyone. But that angel came into the church with us and stayed right by me all the way through the service.

"That was the best day of my life. I married my childhood sweetheart and met my guardian angel on the same day! My wife has never seen him, but believes implicitly in my guardian angel, because he always turns up when we need him."

These are all spontaneous appearances of guardian angels. None of them was anticipated or expected, and, as in most of the examples I have heard about over the years, the person was usually terrified to begin with.

There are many more accounts of people who knew that their guardian angels were present, even though invisible.

One famous example of this concerns the British Antarctic explorer Sir Ernest Shackleton. When he and two companions were making an arduous crossing of the mountains of South Georgia they were always aware of "one more" who traveled with them.[9]

In 1916, during World War I, Commander Stoker and two companions escaped from a Turkish prison. They managed to walk three hundred miles to the Mediterranean and freedom. During the entire trek Commander Stoker was constantly aware that they were being accompanied by an extra person. The men did not discuss this with each other until they reached safety, and then discovered that they had all had the same experience.[10]

Sir Francis Smythe, the mountaineer, is another example. In the final stages of climbing Mount Everest in 1933, his companion was forced to turn back, and Smythe carried on by himself. He had a constant feeling that a silent, friendly and invisible companion was climbing along with him. "In its company," he said, "I could not feel lonely, neither could I come to any harm."[11]

In his book, *Adventures of a Mountaineer*, Smythe wrote:

> *All the time that I was climbing alone, I had the feeling that there was someone with me. I felt also that were I to slip I should be held up and supported as though I had a companion above me with a rope...When I reached the ledge I felt I ought to eat something in order to keep up my strength. All I had brought with me was a slab of Kendal mint cake. This I took out of my pocket and, carefully dividing it into two halves, turned round with one half in my hand to offer to my "companion."*[12]

However, it is also possible to ask guardian angels to reveal themselves. There are a number of ways to do this.

In ancient times when Native Americans reached puberty they were sent out naked to find their guardian spirits.[13] This technique used stress, deprivation, and hardship to encourage the creation of visions. Fortunately, we do not need to do anything as difficult as this to find our guardian angels. In fact, frequently your guardian angel will appear just as soon as you invite your angel into your life.

Here are the ways I have found most effective to encourage your guardian angel.

Invoking the Archangels

You may have wondered why I talked about the archangels in the previous chapter. The archangels have many functions, but one of them is to assist us and help us achieve our goals. If one of your goals is to make contact with your guardian angel, the archangels can help.

With practice, you will be able to invoke the archangels whenever you wish. I have even done it on a crowded subway station in the middle of rush hour. However, make sure that you are alone and unlikely to be disturbed the first time you try this. Have the room at a pleasant temperature. You do not want to be too hot, but neither do you want to be shivering. Disconnect the phone. Play some quiet, soothing, meditation-type music if you wish. Wear comfortable, loose-fitting clothes. Shake your arms and hands vigorously to release any built-up tension. I usually roll my shoulders as well. The stress and tension of the day build up in our upper backs and shoulders, and it is a good idea to let go of this unwanted baggage before taking part in any spiritual work.

Sit down in a comfortable chair, close your eyes and take three deep breaths. As you exhale, say to yourself, "Relax, relax deeply."

Concentrate on your breathing, until you feel that you are beginning to relax. Then let your energies focus on different parts of your body, telling them to relax. I start with my head and face and go down through my neck and shoulders, arms and fingers, abdomen, then legs, until even the tips of my toes are relaxed. Some people prefer to start by relaxing their feet and moving upwards. It makes no difference which method you prefer. The object is simply to become as relaxed as possible.

You may find that you fall asleep doing this exercise, particularly if you are doing it in the evening after a busy day. Do not worry if this happens. Your body obviously needed the rest, so enjoy the sleep and try again later.

Once you feel that your entire body is relaxed, you are ready to invoke the archangels. "Invoke" means "to call upon," usually for help or inspiration. We are calling upon the archangels for help in contacting our guardian angels, and also for inspiration.

Fortunately, it is easy to invoke the archangels. You simply need to accept the fact that they are present and willing to help you.

Start by visualizing the archangel Michael standing on your right side. You can visualize him in any form or shape that you desire. If you have a mental picture of him from childhood days at Sunday school, use that, as it will be easy for you to visualize. If you have no religious background, simply envisage a beautiful angel that represents love.

I see the four archangels as being about eight feet tall, with beautiful faces that look as if they've been sculpted from marble, wearing gorgeous white flowing robes, and with large, folded wings. This picture dates from my childhood and is extremely easy for me to imagine. Other people I have spoken to see the archangels in quite different ways. One of my neighbors sees them as balls of energy and pure light. In his case, they bear no resemblance at all to the traditional pictures of angels, but this visualization works well for him. One lady I know, who has worked a great deal in the Native American tradition, sees the archangels as animal spirits.

As you can see, you have a great deal of flexibility in how you choose to see the archangels. In fact, it is good if you have no preconceived ideas about how they should look. That way, the archangels will present themselves to you in the shape and form that they desire.

It might take several minutes before you feel that archangel Michael is actually standing beside you. Do not worry about this. With practice, you will find that you can invoke him, whenever you wish, in a matter of seconds.

Once you are aware that archangel Michael is standing on your right side, invoke archangel Gabriel. Gabriel will stand on your left-hand side. Gabriel is the angel who helps you overcome doubts and fears, and gives you self-esteem and increased confidence. With Gabriel on your left side you can overcome your fears and achieve anything you wish. I can feel my confidence growing whenever I visualize Gabriel beside me.

You should be feeling invigorated by now. On your right-hand side you have Michael, the angel of love, and on your left, Gabriel, the angel who gives you confidence.

Now it is time to invoke archangel Uriel. Visualize Uriel standing directly in front of you. With Uriel in this position your thinking will become clearer, your concentration and powers of observation will increase, and you will recognize and understand the motivations and actions of others more clearly than ever before.

Finally, invoke archangel Raphael. Raphael, the angel of healing, stands directly behind you. You will be able to sense the strong healing energies as soon as Raphael arrives.

With all four archangels in position you are, in effect, surrounded by a circle of protection and power. It is a wonderful, intense, glorious feeling that you will want to recapture often. And you should. It is extremely beneficial for you in many ways. This rite provides love, confidence, clarity of mind, healing—and total protection!

Amazingly, this ritual is not over yet.

With the four archangels surrounding you, visualize a stream of pure, clear divine light coming down from the heavens, entering your body through your head and revitalizing every nerve, organ, muscle, and fiber of your entire body. There is so much of it that it overflows and completely surrounds you in a huge tunnel of light.

In the Jewish tradition, this light is called *shekinah*, the female principle of God, which is part of the spirit of life that is inside all of us.[14]

Much of the time, simply invoking these four archangels will be sufficient. This ritual will give you confidence when you feel the need for it, make you become aware of the incredible protection that is around you, restore your health and vitality, and grant you the ability to see and understand everything with a new sense of clarity.

However, the archangels will also act on your wishes. Your desires have to be pure and hurtful to no one. I am assuming that the first time you invoke the archangels you will be asking them to help you make contact with your guardian angel.

You may not achieve complete success the first time you invoke the archangels. You may successfully visualize one or two archangels but be unable to contact the others. You may fall asleep or be interrupted. Do not worry if you are unsuccessful for any reason. Practice makes perfect. Let go of any past failures and start completely anew the next time an opportunity arises.

You should feel comfortable with the four archangels surrounding you, and with the *shekinah* light enveloping you in pure love. Once you are experienced at reaching this state you will be able to open your eyes and look around. I do not recommend that you do this until you have performed the ritual several times. This is because the beauty, serenity, purity, and dazzling, almost blinding, light of the archangels is likely to startle you and propel you back into your everyday world. The feeling of loss that accompanies this sensation is indescribable. I know from my own experience that the dull, sick feeling in the pit of my stomach lasts for several hours. Do not open your eyes at any time during this ritual until you are completely familiar with it. There is an unbelievable treat in store for you when you reach this state.

Now it is time to thank the four archangels for coming to you and for their love, guidance, and protection. I like to address each one individually. If the situation allows, I say the following out loud. If this is not possible, for instance, when I am at the subway station, I say the words in my mind.

"Thank you, Michael," I might say. "I know that you are busy and I'm grateful to you for coming to my aid today. Your gift of love will help me become more giving and loving in my life, and for that I am truly grateful. Thank you."

I wait for a response. Occasionally, I might hear words, but usually I simply feel myself enfolded in a gentle, but strong, loving embrace.

"Thank you, Gabriel," I continue after a few moments. "I am grateful to you for coming at my request. I am often fearful, but know that with your help and protection I can do anything. Thank you for giving me confidence and strength."

Again I wait. Gabriel usually responds by allowing me to feel that I really can accomplish anything. I visualize Gabriel as being feminine, but on the few occasions words have been said to me, they have been in a deep, resonant voice.

"Thank you, Uriel, for giving me clarity of mind. You are busy, too, and I appreciate you coming to my aid. I function best when my mind is clear and open. Thank you for your help."

Uriel usually responds to me with a feeling of warmth, particularly on my eyelids. It lasts only a few seconds, but is extremely comforting.

"Thank you, Raphael, for your powers of healing. You restore every part of my body and enable me to help restore others as well. I am very grateful. Thank you for coming to my aid today."

Raphael responds by giving me a strong sense of physical well-being. I feel tireless and full of unlimited energy after speaking with Raphael.

"Thank you all," I continue. "Today I need your help in a different way." At this point I ask the archangels for whatever it is I want. The first time you do this you will probably want to contact your guardian angel. Consequently, you will say something like this: "I have not yet met or made proper contact with my guardian angel. Please help me. I know I have a guardian angel, and although I sometimes feel the protection around me, I want to know more. Please help me meet my guardian angel."

Once you have made your request, pause and simply become aware of yourself and the archangels. Visualize the *shekinah* light surrounding you all. When the time is right, and this may be just a few seconds or as long as several minutes, say, "Thank you," preferably out loud, and open your eyes. Remain confident that your request will be attended to.

You will find that you look at the world completely differently for several hours after conducting this ritual. Everything will seem richer, and you will see with a new clarity. Your relationships with others will be smoother, your stress levels will decrease, and you'll experience a sense of quiet confidence. If you do the ritual shortly before going to bed you will enjoy the best night's sleep you have had for ages.

You may have to perform this ritual several times before your guardian angel arrives. Of course, your guardian angel is around you all the time. However, like most people, you may not have been aware of this.

Experiencing Your Guardian Angel

Many people expect guardian angels to appear before them dressed in flowing robes, surrounded by light, and holding a harp. This could happen, but it is unlikely.

Knowing

You may gradually feel a sense of increased protection, a certain knowing that your guardian angel is protecting you.

This happened to a friend of mine. After being widowed at an early age she gradually retreated into her small apartment. After a few years it became her prison and she was scared to venture outside. Everything was delivered and left outside her door. She would not open the door until the delivery person had left. Once she became aware of her guardian angel she began venturing outside again. She is still more timid than most people, but at least she is now leading a normal life, and her confidence is growing more and more, thanks to the help of her guardian angel.

Dreams

You may experience your guardian angel in your dreams. This is very common. After all, our dreams help us evaluate what is happening in our lives, so that we can make sense of what is going on and function adequately. If you find your guardian angel appears in this way, place a notebook and pen beside your bed so that you can write down everything you remember as soon as you wake up. As you know, our dreams tend to fade away and be forgotten as soon as we start on our daily routine.

It is a good idea to keep a dream diary, anyway, as it enables you to get valuable insights into what your subconscious mind is working on. Your dreams can also provide glimpses into the future. This allows you to take the correct actions at the right time and make your life as successful as possible.

Thoughts and Feelings

Thoughts and feelings are other ways our guardian angels speak to us. Skeptics might say that we all have thoughts and feelings all the time, and this is true. Obviously, every thought or feeling does not come from our guardian angels. However, every now and again, when a thought or feeling occurs to us we know instinctively that it has come from another source, and not from our subconscious minds.

Many creative people experience this feeling regularly. I believe this other source to be the guardian angel. Naturally, it pays to give special attention to these thoughts and feelings.

A highly successful businessman I know told me that he feels a special warmth whenever such thoughts or feelings come to him. "I know then that I'm on the right track," he said. "If I follow the feeling I'll make the right decision. If I ignore it, I always regret it later on."

Intuition

Closely related to our feelings are intuitive hunches. We all experience these from time to time. Are these messages from our angel guardians? I would have to say "yes."

Interestingly enough, we can sometimes receive these hunches and not be consciously aware of them. Many years ago, William E. Cox, a parapsychologist, conducted a statistical experiment using the passengers who traveled on certain trains. He wanted to compare the number of people on trains that were involved in accidents to the number of people on trains that arrived safely at their destinations. He obtained the number of passengers traveling on a certain route seven, fourteen, twenty-one, and twenty-eight days before the same train was involved in an accident. The statistical tables he derived from this information showed that passengers did somehow manage to avoid accident-bound trains. They did not avoid these trains deliberately. However, on the days when an accident occurred they slept in, decided to have a day off work, or simply missed the train. In eleven train accidents, seven carried fewer passengers than they had on the previous day. Six carried fewer passengers than they had on the same day a week earlier, and four of them transported fewer passengers on the fateful day than they had on any of the previous eight days.

His statistics about Pullman passengers were even more interesting. Cox assumed that these people would have booked their seats ahead of time. However, his statistics showed that in seventeen train accidents involving Pullman passengers, ten of the trains carried fewer passengers than they had on the same day a week earlier. Also, five of the trains had fewer passengers on the day of the accident than they had on any day in the previous week.

Cox extended his research to examine thirty-five accidents and found that similar results applied to eighty percent of the accidents.[15]

Why did these people miss the trains on the fateful days? The odds are far too great to be put down simply to chance. Is it too far-fetched to believe that the passengers who missed the train were somehow warned or protected by their guardian angels?

Praying

Praying is yet another way of making contact with your guardian angel. Of course, the Bible warns about worshipping angels (Col. 2:18 and Rev. 19:10). However, we are not going to do that. Simply pray in your normal manner, and in the course of the prayer ask for help in contacting your guardian angel. As mentioned earlier, Pope Pius XI used to pray to his guardian angel every night and morning. He would also pray to his guardian angel during the day when he felt it necessary.

Coincidences, Synchronicity, and Serendipity

An old joke goes: "Do you believe in coincidences?"

"No."

"Neither do I. Isn't that a coincidence?"

I believe that coincidences, synchronicity, and serendipity are all examples of our guardian angels at work.

In 1982 I was intending to buy a word processor. Up until then I had been using a manual typewriter, so this purchase was a giant leap forward. I looked at everything that was available at the time and settled on a word processor that allowed me to see the line I had just typed in a small display. When I pressed the return key the machine would then print it and allow me to start on the next line. This seems rather primitive today, but it was many stages ahead of what I had been used to. I decided to buy it. As the salesman offered me a small discount for cash, I headed for the bank and withdrew the money I needed. Over the previous few months I had become friendly with the teller and told him what the money was for.

"You shouldn't buy one of those," he told me. "A computer will do a hundred times more than that and cost about the same amount of money."

I had not even considered a computer. In fact, the thought of one terrified me.

"I'm about to have my lunch. I'll show you one of the computers we have here."

He kindly gave me a demonstration in the bank. He convinced me and I went out and bought my first computer.

A number of things convince me that my guardian angel was behind this.

1. I have never, before or since, told a bank teller why I was withdrawing cash.

2. I try to get along well with everyone, but this man was the only bank teller with whom I have ever become really friendly.

3. I was fortunate that this teller knew something about computers.

4. It was also extremely fortunate for me that he was enthusiastic about computers and was prepared to give up part of his lunch hour to give me a demonstration. It was also fortunate that I happened to be served by him just before he stopped for his lunch break.

5. By buying the computer I was able to write more quickly and effectively than ever. Consequently, I began to take my writing more seriously.

Letter Writing

A particularly powerful way of making contact with your guardian angel is to write a letter. Start, "Dear Guardian Angel," and then simply write down everything you wish to say. You might write something simple along these lines:

Dear Guardian Angel,

I am aware that you are around me, protecting and guiding me, every day of my life, but now I wish to get to know you better. Please make contact so that we can become closer. Thank you.

Love from (your name)

Some people I know write regular letters to their guardian angels and these can be several pages long. You can make your letters to your guardian angel as personal as you like as no one will see it, except for you and your angel.

Once the letter is written, place it in an envelope, address it "To My Guardian Angel," seal it—and then burn it. Make a ceremony of it. Believe that you are burning it to send it directly to your angel. Collect the ashes and scatter them out of doors. I prefer to do the whole process outside. I have a personal "oracle tree,"[16] and sit beneath it to write letters to my guardian angel. I then burn the paper under the tree and let the ashes be blown away by a breeze. As with the other methods, remain confident that your angel will receive the letter and make contact with you.

Draw Your Guardian Angel

All forms of creativity can be enhanced when you call on your guardian angel for help. However, you can also use your creativity to find your guardian angel.

Experiment by drawing pictures of angels and coloring them in. It makes no difference what the quality of your artwork is. A cousin of mine was able to make a career as a professional artist, but I am hopeless at drawing and painting. However, I draw angels for myself and no one else sees them.

When you focus on drawing angels you attract your guardian angel to you. You may find your guardian angel gradually influencing the movements of your pen, and find yourself creating something beautiful.

Be Open and Aware

A highly effective way of making contact with your guardian angel is to remain open and aware. Realize that your guardian angel is there and wants to help. In fact, one of the quickest ways to make contact with your guardian angel is simply to call out: "Help!" Naturally, you should not do this except when absolutely necessary.

Speak to your guardian angel. Ask for whatever you need. Make your requests as clear as possible. If you are not sure what you want you will not be able to ask for it correctly. Getting into the habit of making your requests clear and concise is a valuable one. Knowing what you want is an essential part of the process. If you don't know what you want, how will you know when you've got it? Ask your guardian angel to provide whatever it is you need. Remain calm, positive and confident that your angel will do whatever is necessary to obtain it for you.

It can be very useful to have regular conversations with your guardian angel. Ask for the things you need, but also tell your angel what is going on in your life. Talk about your successes and achievements and those of your loved ones. Tell your guardian angel when you are happy, stressed, lonely, or bored. Regular communication like this makes it much easier for your guardian angel to become a vital part of your life. Do not expect rapid results, though this could well happen. Be patient, and keep talking.

It is a good habit to thank your angel every night for looking after you and helping you. We all like being thanked, and angels are no exceptions.

Creating Your Guardian Angel

This method is a highly practical one that produces excellent results. We will practice this in the next chapter.

Your Guardian Angel's Name

Once you have made contact with your guardian angel ask for his or her name. This is important in many ways. Knowing someone's name immediately makes you that much closer to the person. It provides a rapport that is essential for deeper communication. I am sure you remember the old German fairy tale, *Rumpelstiltskin*. That story certainly demonstrates the power that a name possesses.

Knowing your guardian angel's name gives you instant access, as you simply need to say it for your angel to be in your consciousness.

You may find the name comes spontaneously when you first make contact. Do not worry if it takes a while. Simply meditate, or do a progressive relaxation, and ask for it. The name will then appear in your mind.

3

Creating Your Guardian Angel

I have found this method particularly useful for people who have had difficulty in contacting their guardian angel in the other ways. However, you will enjoy creating your guardian angel in this way, even if you have been successful with the methods in chapter 2.

We create our own reality in life. This is usually not a conscious process, of course, though psychologists have demonstrated that we have the power to change our lives by changing our thoughts. As we create our own reality, we can also create anything we need to make our lives as full and meaningful as possible.

Your thoughts have incredible power and manifest everything that happens in your life. Have you ever walked into a room where someone was enthusiastic and full of life? I am sure you were caught up in the happiness and joyfulness of that person. I am sure you have also walked into a situation where someone was angry. Did you respond to that person's thoughts and feelings?

Telepathy occurs when someone picks up what someone else is thinking. Obviously, the person transmitting that thought has put energy and power into it, to enable it to be picked up by someone else. There have been many recorded instances of shared dreams: someone's dream is picked up by someone else who is also dreaming.[1] Obviously, the person who dreams the dream first is transmitting energies that are subconsciously picked up by the second dreamer. If we can send out energies from our dreams without even knowing it, we can consciously send out energy from our thoughts—"daydreams," if you wish—in the same way.

Carl Jung described angels as "nothing but the thoughts and intuitions of their Lord."[2] This quote indicates that Jung believed God was creating angels by using thought and intuition. This is what you will be doing if you follow the exercises in this chapter. Thomas Aquinas appeared to believe that angels were thought forms when he wrote: "Angels are composed of the ambient air of the place where they appear, which they arrange and condense into an appropriate form."[3] In his book, *A Dictionary of Angels*,

Gustav Davidson wrote: "I am prepared to say if enough of us believe in angels, the angels exist."[4]

A prayer is a good example of someone deliberately sending out thoughts and feelings. People who pray would not bother to do so if they did not believe their prayers would be heard. The person praying is creating what the Theosophists call a thought form.

Thought forms are small parcels of concentrated energy. We all have some fifty to sixty thousand thoughts a day. You could picture these as thousands of small parcels attached to a long piece of rope. However, most of the time we have no control over our thoughts. We think of something, which leads us on to something else, which in turn reminds us of something we should have done yesterday, and so on.

For instance, if we are eating a particular chocolate, we may suddenly remember eating the same type of chocolate with a close friend. Then our thoughts might suddenly change to when we were five years old and we gazed at a beautiful display of tempting chocolates in a department store. From there, we might go to an occasion when we ate too many chocolates and ended up being ill, and so on.

There is an internal logic to our thoughts, but most of them would be extremely boring to an outside person who happened to tune in on what we were thinking. Of course, this is unlikely, as we usually pick up only those thoughts that have energy or emotion attached to them. Prayers, for instance, are often made when a person desperately needs help or comfort. Obviously, there is considerable energy involved, and this creates a powerful thought form.

Thought forms generally are not visible to others, but in many recorded instances they have been. In her book *Psychic Self-Defence*, Dion Fortune discusses a situation in which mentally ill people complained about being attacked by invisible beings. The doctors and psychologists considered this to be further proof of the patients' insanity, but psychics were able to see the attacking entities. "Does this mean that the psychic is mistaken in thinking he perceives an astral entity?" Fortune wrote. "In my opinion both psychic and psychologist are right, and their findings are mutually explanatory. What the psychic sees is the dissociated complex extruded from the aura as a thought form."[5]

Charles Dickens' characters were so powerfully created in his mind that they became thought forms who followed him everywhere. James T. Fields said: "He (Charles Dickens) told me that when he was writing *The Old Curiosity Shop* the creatures of his imagination haunted him so much that they would neither let him sleep or eat in peace."[6]

Constructing a Thought Form

There are a number of things we need to create a powerful thought form.

Emotion

We are emotional beings and tend to attach feelings to our thoughts. In fact, if there is no emotion attached to the thought it is usually discarded quickly. You can test this by deliberately thinking about a negative experience you had as a small child. As you think about it, you will find all the emotions that occurred coming back, even though the experience may have happened decades ago. Now think about something unimportant that happened yesterday. As it was unimportant, it will probably be hard to think of anything. Because there were no emotions attached, the incident faded away and was forgotten.

This is part of the body's natural protection system. If we remained aware of absolutely everything that happened to us all the time, we would quickly become overloaded and unable to function. Consequently, all the unimportant things are barely noticed and frequently do not even reach our conscious awareness.

To create a thought form we need to put emotion into it to make it vivid and memorable. In fact, the more emotion we put into it, the greater the effect will be.

Think about something really exciting and memorable in your life. Perhaps it was meeting someone special, or being honored in some way. Because emotion is attached to these memories, they carry much energy and intensity, and these feelings remain with you for the rest of your life.

Mental Imaging

We need to be able to picture clearly the thought form we are creating. If we have no idea what it is we are going to create, we will not know when we have achieved it. Any doubts, confusion or hesitation destroy the thought form even before it has been created.

I am sure you have met people who can never get out exactly what they want to say. Assuming they do not have a speech impediment, this will be because they have not thought the matter through properly before starting to speak. If your thoughts are well defined and you can picture them clearly in your mind, you will be able to focus and concentrate on them.

Relaxation

We need to be calm and relaxed to construct a thought form consciously. If you are worried or preoccupied about something, you need to resolve the situation or put it aside before starting.

We also need a calm, pleasant, relaxing environment to work in. It is hard to concentrate on building up a thought form if people are arguing in the next room, or the room is too hot or cold. Choose a suitable time, when the situation is as near perfect as possible, to work on these exercises.

The Law of Attraction

We must remain aware that our thoughts attract what we think about. If we think negative thoughts most of the time, we attract negativity into our lives. If we think poverty, guess what happens? We develop a poverty consciousness and become a magnet that attracts poverty. If we deliberately think of abundance, we will attract abundance into our lives. When we think positive, happy thoughts, we attract like-minded, positive, happy people into our lives.

We can do this consciously, by becoming aware of our thoughts and changing any unwanted thoughts as soon as we become aware of them. You can literally change your life by doing this. If you are thinking mainly negative thoughts, you will notice an incredible difference as soon as you start consciously changing them into positive thoughts. Instead of attracting lack, restrictions and limitations into your life, you will suddenly start attracting abundance and well-being. This will have a powerful positive effect in every area of your life. We need to be careful when consciously creating thought forms to send out only good, positive thoughts and emotions.

Creating Your Guardian Angel

Now it is time to start creating your guardian angel.

1. Ensure that the room is the right temperature and that you will not be disturbed. Take the phone off the hook and close the blinds or curtains.

2. You may wish to burn a little incense and/or light four white candles. If you use candles, place one in each of the four directions and sit in the middle. If it makes you more comfortable, play some meditation-type music. It is not a good idea to play recognizable songs or an album of one of your favorite

singers, because these are likely to be distracting. However, a New Age, relaxation, or stress-reducing tape can be helpful.

3. Wear loose-fitting clothes. You want to feel as loose and relaxed as possible, so wear something comfortable that does not restrict you in any way.

4. Sit or lie in a comfortable chair. A recliner chair is perfect for this. A bed is not usually a good idea, as you do not want to fall asleep while performing the exercise. I have done that myself a number of times, and now always do this exercise in a relaxed sitting position, rather than lying down completely.

5. Once you are as comfortable as possible, close your eyes. This is done for a number of reasons. By eliminating one of the senses you heighten the others. Also, it is much easier to visualize something with your eyes closed. This also eliminates any potential distractions that could be caused if your eyes suddenly noticed something in the room.

6. Allow all your muscles to become as relaxed as possible. I normally use the progressive relaxation technique described in the next chapter to achieve this, but any method that works for you will do.

   One good method is to tense all the muscles in one arm, then let go and allow them to relax. Continue with the other arm and each of your legs, and then tell your body, neck, and head to relax.

Another method is to extend your arms in front of you, take a deep breath, and count backwards from five to one as you exhale. When you reach "one," let your arms drop loosely into your lap and say to yourself, "relax." With a little practice you will find yourself becoming totally relaxed in a matter of seconds using this method.

7. Become aware of the stillness and quietness around you. Go through your entire body mentally to see if you are completely relaxed. If any part is not as relaxed as it could be, focus your energies on it and tell it to relax.

8. Once you are completely relaxed, picture the back of your right hand in your imagination. If you are left-handed, picture your left hand. See it as completely as possible. Mentally turn the hand over so you can see the palm vividly in your mind's eye. Picture the main lines and the tiny skin ridge patterns. See your hand for the wonder and miracle that it is.

   Turn the hand over, focus on your thumb, and gradually concentrate on the thumbnail. Allow your thumbnail to fill the picture in your mind completely. This nail will be the screen on which you project your thought form.

9. Picture in your mind your guardian angel. This may not be easy to do at first, and you are likely to find your mind drifting off on all sorts of tangents. When you find this happening, simply visualize your thumbnail again, and then picture your guardian angel. It is important that you stay relaxed. Our minds are inclined to wander, so there is no need to berate yourself when this happens. Simply go back and visualize your thumbnail again.

10. We all have different pictures of what our guardian angel looks like. You might picture a cute little cherub, or perhaps a tall angel dressed in beautiful robes. Your guardian angel may simply be a bright light that expresses ineffable love. Your angel may, or may not, have wings. In fact, it might simply be an impression, an awareness that your angel is there. Use your imagination and let your inner mind conjure up a picture for you.

    None of us can escape our backgrounds and upbringing. If you come from a religious family your image of your guardian angel is likely to be a traditional one, dazzlingly white, with large wings and flowing robes. If you have no spiritual background your image could be completely different. It makes no difference. Simply visualize it as fully as possible.

11. Once you have an impression of your guardian angel in your mind it is time to turn this picture into a

thought form. Let the picture of your guardian angel disappear and be replaced by an image of your thumbnail. Once you can clearly see your thumbnail, switch back, as quickly as you can, to the image of your guardian angel. Do this several times. You will find that it will become faster and easier each time you do it.

12. At this stage you start to invest the image of your guardian angel with emotion. Think of a particularly happy time in your life, when you felt yourself surrounded by security and love. If you have never experienced these feelings in your own life, simply imagine what it must be like. Allow these feelings to surround you completely, so that your entire being is enveloped with the energy of pure love.

    With these strong emotions pervading your being, visualize your guardian angel again. Because of the practice you had in switching at the previous stage, this should be easy to do.

    Again, do this several times. Allow the picture of your guardian angel to fade and be replaced with feelings of perfect love. When they completely surround you, switch back to a picture of your guardian angel. What you are doing here is imprinting the strong emotion of perfect love into your image of your guardian angel.

13. At this stage simply observe your guardian angel. You may find the picture becoming much clearer in your mind. You might feel your angel reflecting love back to you. Your angel may start to get a life of his or her own and surprise you with what he or she does. All these things are positive and you can congratulate yourself on what you have achieved.

14. In this final stage you set your guardian angel free to come and go as required. Your guardian angel has been constructed in a sense by your imagination and visualization, but you have added consciousness and love. Both your creation and a part of the universe, the angel is part of you, but also has individuality. Consequently, although acting in your best interests all the time, the angel may not always do what you wish.

    Become aware of your thumbnail again and gradually widen the view until you can see your hand clearly. Turn it over in your mind so that the palm is facing upwards. Visualize your guardian angel standing on the palm of your hand. Large or small, your guardian angel can still fit on the palm of your hand.

    In your mind, thank your guardian angel for being there. Surround the angel with love and watch the love being absorbed. Finally, again in your mind, slowly bring your open palm up to your lips and blow gently. Watch your angel lift off the palm of your hand and fly upwards.

15. Spend a few moments in quiet contemplation before returning to your everyday world. Come back slowly by counting from one to five. When you reach five, open your eyes, stretch, and when you feel ready, get up.

You probably will be unable to complete this exercise on the first, or even first half-dozen, attempts. It makes no difference how long it takes; you will get further into the exercise every time you do it.

But Is It Real?

I would love to know how many times I have been asked this question. I usually answer it with another question: "Does your guardian angel seem real?"

The answer is always "yes."

"Does your constructed guardian angel look after your best interests?"

Again, the answer is "yes."

"Do you feel the comfort, warmth, and protection that you should experience from a guardian angel?"

"Yes."

"In that case, does it matter if your constructed guardian angel is real or not?"

"No."

However, I personally believe that a constructed guardian angel is real. By creating a thought form, we have created a living parcel of vibrant, loving, healing and nurturing energy. That thought form is real, as real as the chair I am sitting on.

Carl Jung said that angels personify "the coming into consciousness of something new arising from the deep unconscious." Isn't that exactly what you have done by creating your own guardian angel?

Peter Lamborn Wilson wrote: "When man opens his heart, for even an instant, the figure he perceives (or the intuition he receives) is his Guardian Angel."[7] Joel Goldsmith told us "not to place faith in the outer world, but always to turn within and become better acquainted with our guardian angel, the angel of the Lord...which has been planted in the midst of us since the beginning of all time."[8] We do these two things in this experiment.

You can create thought forms for anything you wish. In her book, *Magic and Mystery in Tibet*, Alexandra David-Neel chose to create "a most insignificant character: a monk, short and fat, of an innocent and jolly type." It took her about three months to create her monk, and he then took on a life of his own. At one time, a herdsman brought her a gift of some butter and saw the monk in her tent. He "took it for a live lama." Eventually, this monk became troublesome and David-Neel had to "dissolve" him.[9] Her experience shows that you need to be careful what you ask for. It is perfectly safe to create a guardian angel, but I would think very carefully before trying to create anything else.

It is a valuable exercise to send out thought forms of love, healing, and forgiveness regularly. The people you send these thought forms to will not necessarily know they were sent by you, but they will experience and appreciate the benefits, and you will experience the joy and satisfaction of doing something good and worthwhile.

4

Working With the Archangels

You now know something about the archangels and how to invoke them. Doing this on a regular basis will help you enormously in all areas of your life.

However, there will be times when you need just one archangel. The one you will relate to most easily is the one corresponding to your horoscope sign:

Michael: Aries, Leo, Sagittarius.

Gabriel: Cancer, Scorpio, Pisces.

Raphael: Gemini, Libra, Aquarius.

Uriel: Taurus, Virgo, Capricorn.

This does not mean that you cannot contact one of the other archangels when you wish. However, the one who resonates most to you and your energies will always be the one corresponding to your horoscope sign.

Your angel guardian is with you all the time to help and protect you. Why, then, would you need to invoke one of the archangels?

You might have a special goal that needs extra power or help. It might be something challenging that stretches you to the utmost. We all need to move outside our comfort zones every now and again and tackle something that might even terrify us. By doing this we grow as people.

An acquaintance of mine works as a stand-up comedian. Every night, before he goes on stage, he wishes he had never taken up comedy as a career. He sweats, has butterflies in his stomach, and is convinced that the audience will hate him. But then, the instant he walks onto the stage he is transformed, and when his performance goes well he feels like a million dollars for the rest of the night. Of course, every now and again, he dies on stage, and this possibility is what terrifies him before each performance. My friend is a Leo and finds his pre-show jitters are much less pronounced now that he is in contact with archangel Michael. "I believe Michael could completely eliminate my nerves," he told me. "But I don't want that. I need to feel a little bit nervous to do my best once I'm in front of the audience."

So, if you need extra power or extra protection, summon the correct archangel to your aid.

Each archangel has special responsibilities:

Michael provides protection and patience when we most need it. He can also protect us when we are attacked by others. This can range from verbal criticism to actual physical assault.

Gabriel provides hope, love, intuition, and spirituality. When we desire these qualities, Gabriel can provide them in abundance.

Raphael provides creativity and healing. This nurturing archangel can help restore your physical body to vibrant life. Raphael can also increase your creative output. If you are thinking of doing something artistic or creative, Raphael can stop you from procrastinating and help you achieve something worthwhile.

Uriel provides insight, clarity, and vision. If you feel you are not seeing the whole picture, or are failing to understand people's hidden motivations, call on Uriel to help you see what is going on.

We can summon an archangel in many different ways. The first method uses a progressive relaxation technique.

Method One

If you have not done this before, you will find the experience highly beneficial, as every cell in your body is allowed to relax. This should happen naturally when we sleep at night but often it doesn't. If you have ever awakened in the morning feeling as if you need an extra few hours of rest, it means different parts of your body have been tense even though you were asleep. You can provide relaxation, which each cell of your body needs to function correctly, through regular sessions of progressive relaxation.

You may find it helpful to tape the following script so that you can simply close your eyes and listen.

Start by ensuring you will not be disturbed. This may mean that you temporarily disconnect the phone. Ensure that the room is warm, or cover yourself with a blanket. Lie down or sit back in a comfortable chair and concentrate on relaxing. Here is the script that I use:

"Take a nice deep breath in and gently close your eyes as you exhale. Allow that pleasant relaxation to flow through every part of your body. Nothing need disturb or bother you now as you drift into this pleasant world of total rest and relaxation.

"Each breath you take makes you more and more relaxed. You can feel the stress and tension fading away until you feel like a loose, limp rag doll.

"Take another deep breath now, and as you exhale, feel the tension leaving every part of your head and face. It's a wonderful feeling to relax in this way.

"Take another deep breath, and as you exhale, feel the stress and tension leaving your neck. It's so comfortable and feels so good.

"Take another deep breath, and this time, as you exhale, feel all the tension leaving your shoulders. Allow the tension to leave your arms, your hands, your fingers.

"Each breath you take from now on will allow the stress and tension and strain to leave every part of your body. Feel it leaving your chest and stomach now. It feels so comfortable that you have no desire to move. You just want to enjoy the feeling of this wonderful relaxation as it spreads throughout your body, revitalizing every cell of your being.

"Feel your legs relaxing now. The muscles in your thighs and calves are letting go now. Your feet and even your toes are relaxing more and more.

"You feel totally relaxed, but you can go even deeper now. Feel a beam of energy go right through your body, starting at the top of your head and drifting down. Everywhere it finds tension or stress or strain or tightness, it will focus on it and allow it to relax. Feel this beam of energy as it steadily examines and relaxes every part of your body.

"Now you are relaxed, and every breath you take makes you even more relaxed, making you feel loose, limp, and totally receptive to the words you are going to hear now.

"To begin, in your mind's eye, imagine the most beautiful staircase in the world. You may be fortunate enough to have seen this staircase somewhere in the past. If so, picture it clearly in your mind. If you don't have an actual staircase in mind, simply imagine the most beautiful staircase you can.

"Imagine what the banister looks like as you rest your hand on it. Feel the texture of the carpet or cool marble beneath your feet. Imagine if the staircase goes straight down or has a graceful curve to it. Picture in your mind the beautiful room that it leads down to. You are about to go down that staircase now, and a wave of excitement passes through you as you realize that you are about to see archangel Michael (or the archangel you wish to contact).

"Take the first step down the staircase now, and double your relaxation as you do so.

"Double your relaxation again as you take another step. Keep on doing this as you slowly descend the staircase.

"Visualize yourself on the staircase as you head downward to your meeting with your archangel.

"Feel yourself reach the floor. Pause and look around. The room is the most magnificent you have ever seen. You might want to walk around and familiarize yourself with this fabulous room. Try sitting down in a comfortable chair and notice how you just sink into the soft cushions. Feel the richness of the materials, the brocade, and notice all the gorgeous rich colors.

"You feel so comfortable in this room. At one end is a large door. It is the most magnificent door you have ever seen. There is a name carved on the door—the name of your archangel. You decide to go over and knock on this door, but as you do the door slowly opens and out comes your archangel."

(You will see your archangel in a form that is perfect for you. Many people see a ball of pure, shining light rather than a person. Some people cannot really make out the shape of the archangel at all because of the brightness that surrounds him or her. Thomas Aquinas believed that angels are pure thoughts, and that even their bodies were created from thought.[1] Because of this, you may even see your archangel as a thought, rather than as a being. It makes no difference how you see your archangel. Know that it will be determined by your background and religious upbringing, and that any form is perfect.)

"You greet your archangel in a manner that seems appropriate to you. You find your archangel friendly, warm and engaging. You enjoy a pleasant conversation, and now you ask your questions.

"See yourself asking them and now see yourself hearing the replies. (Pause.)

"And now your archangel is ready to leave. See yourself giving your thanks and watching as the door slowly closes again. You are now alone once more in this beautiful room.

"Sit down comfortably in one of the chairs and just allow yourself to drift even deeper for a moment or two. (Pause.)

"And now it is time to return to your everyday life. On the count of five you will open your eyes feeling completely energized and revitalized. You will remember absolutely everything that happened, and you will be ready to face the world again with increased confidence.

"One. Gaining energy and feeling wonderful.

"Two. Feeling at peace with yourself and the world.

"Three. Totally revitalized and full of energy.

"Four. Aware of your special talents and abilities.

"And five. Opening your eyes and feeling fantastic."

I find it helpful to write down my insights immediately after a session while everything is still clear in my mind.

You will find that after you have done progressive relaxations for a while, you will be able to speed things up by starting your relaxation from the top of the staircase. Once you start receiving good results from this, you will then be able to simply close your eyes, count from five down to one, and instantly be inside your special room. Do not be in a hurry to achieve this. Although I can be inside my room in a matter of seconds, I frequently prefer to spend time in getting there, as it gives me an opportunity to let go of everything that has happened to me during the day.

Method Two

This second method is not as reliable as the first, but I know many people who have good results with it.

Again, sit back in a comfortable chair and close your eyes. Imagine that the archangel you are invoking is standing directly in front of you. See if you can picture him or her clearly in your mind. It may take a minute or two before the picture becomes clear. Once it does, picture everything in vivid detail. Look closely at the archangel's face and notice the love and tenderness revealed there. Look at the hair and the clothes. See everything in full color. Notice the radiance surrounding your archangel.

Not everyone can visualize clearly, so you may find it takes several attempts to get the results you want. Once you can see the archangel with perfect clarity, ask for whatever it is you need. Usually, once your request has been made, the archangel will gradually fade from sight. Sometimes you may feel a slight pressure on your shoulders, as if the archangel is gently patting you before leaving. Say "thank you," preferably out loud, before the vision disappears completely.

Take a few seconds to become familiar with your surroundings and then open your eyes.

Method Three

Many of my students tell me that they enjoy this method more than the others. I have no personal preference, but always have good results with this method. I call it the Archangel Color Meditation.

We each have a special color that radiates to us. If you have a favorite color and receive plenty of compliments whenever you wear it, that is likely to be the correct color for this method.

If you do not have a color that immediately leaps to mind, you can find the correct color for you by using numerology. All you have to do is turn your full date of birth into a number and then relate that number to the correct color. You start by creating a sum from the month, day, and full year of birth. Here is an example of someone born on April 28, 1980:

4

28

+ 1980

2012

These numbers are then reduced to a single digit: 2+0+1+2 = 5.

Unfortunately, there are two exceptions. If your numbers total either 11 or 22 at any stage in the reducing process, stop there, and do not reduce down to a single digit. These two numbers are known as Master Numbers or Life Path Numbers in numerology.[2] Here is an example:

2

29

+ 1944

1975 and 1+9+7+5 = 22.

We create a sum out of the date of birth so that we do not lose the 11s or 22s. For instance, the example above reduced down to 22 by creating a sum. If we add up the numbers in a long row, we end up losing the 22:

2 (month) +2+9 (day) +1+9+4+4 (year) = 31, and 3+1 = 4.

Once you have reduced your date of birth to a single digit (or 11 or 22) you will have found what is known as your Life Path Number in numerology. Now you can determine your color from this list:

1 = Red	*5 = Blue*	*9 = Bronze*
2 = Orange	*6 = Indigo*	*11 = Silver*
3 = Yellow	*7 = Purple*	*22 = Gold*[3]
4 = Green	*8 = Pink*	

Now that you know your color, all you need do is sit down and relax totally. You might find it helpful to go through the progressive relaxation exercise used in Method One. Once you are completely relaxed you have a choice. You can visualize yourself completely surrounded and immersed in your color. Alternatively, you might choose to imagine yourself walking through a rainbow until you reach your color.

Either way, you end up totally surrounded by your color. Imagine that you actually are this color. Visualize it growing larger and larger until it fills the room you are in. Then visualize it filling the building, the street, the block, the town, the state, the country, the world, and finally the universe.

Sense the archangel you want to contact. You may choose to contact all four at once, but it is more usual to use this method to contact one at a time. You will feel the presence of the archangel growing as he or she comes close to you.

Keep your eyes closed, but visualize the archangel as clearly as you can. Then simply start talking. Tell the archangel everything that is going on in your life, good and bad. Talk about your hopes and plans. It will be just like talking to your closest friend. You may or may not receive answers from the archangel. You will certainly gain self-esteem, confidence, and love from the experience.

Ask any questions you may have. Again, you may or may not receive an answer. Do not be concerned if no answers come immediately. They will in the next few days, possibly in the form of a dream or as a sudden thought that comes from nowhere. However, you will know that the thought has come directly from the archangel.

If you do not know your guardian angel's name, this is a good time to ask the archangel to tell you. You may find that your guardian angel appears by your side as you are talking with your archangel. This is a good sign. Your guardian angel is there all the time, of course, but it is always pleasant to be reminded of this.

When your conversation is over, thank the archangel. You will sense the archangel fading away, and you will be entirely bathed in your color. Visualize the healing energies of this color washing over the entire universe. Feel it in every pore of your being. When you are ready, thank the universal life force for allowing you the opportunity to spread goodness throughout the universe. Slowly count up to five and open your eyes.

Most people experience a profound sense of well-being after this meditation. It is a spiritual, mystical experience that allows you to unload all of your problems, express healing energies, and see the world anew.

Method Four

I have had mixed results with this method, but include it for the sake of completeness. Simply close your eyes for a few moments and take three deep breaths. Each time you inhale, say to yourself the name of the archangel you are invoking. As you exhale, say, "Come to me."

After saying this three times, open your eyes, and you will find your archangel standing in front of you. I find that the success of this method depends largely on your need at the time. If your need is great, you can virtually guarantee that the archangel will appear. However, if your need is not urgent, the archangel is unlikely to arrive.

This can be frustrating, as something that we consider to be important may be considered frivolous by the archangels. They possess insights and powers that we do not have, and are emotionally detached and impersonal. If your archangel does not appear, think again about your need. Try to put your feelings and emotions to one side and look at the matter in as rational a way as possible. If you still feel that you need to consult an archangel after doing this, do an invocation using one of the other methods. Alternatively, your guardian angel might be sufficient to help you resolve the problem.

5

Ministries of Healing

Imagine being constantly filled with vibrant energy and enthusiasm. You would have a strong sense of purpose and enjoy every moment of this incarnation. Wouldn't life be wonderful? For many people this sounds like an impossible dream, but you can make it happen in your own life with the help of your guardian angel. Your angel can help you heal your mind, body, and spirit. As this happens you will also improve the life of everyone else whose life touches yours.

You can also help heal other people. There is an old prayer that says:

> *May the healing power of Jesus Christ descend upon* (your friend's name) *and may the holy angels encompass him (or her).*

This prayer activates Raphael and the other healing angels to come to your friend's aid. It provides additional support for your friend's guardian angel, and allows spiritual and angelic healing to take place.

The interesting thing is that your friend need have no faith or belief for this to work. I prefer to let people know when I am sending help in this way, but there have been times when this has been impossible. If your friend is unconscious, for instance, you cannot wait for his or her permission, but need to respond immediately.

If you have the time, sit down and perform a progressive relaxation. Imagine your friend lying on a bed in front of you. Visualize the beating of his or her heart, and see the blood flowing to every part of the body. Become attuned to all the energies surrounding your friend, and search out areas of disease. You may find this location by sensing a blockage, a disharmony, or perhaps a break in the rhythm of the body's functions. Send healing energies to this area. Once you have done this, call on Raphael to send angels to assist your friend to recover.

Then send a telepathic message to your friend. Ask your friend to relax and become aware of the healing energies around him or her. Ask your friend to let go of any hurts, grievances, jealousies, or other emotions that may have helped cause the illness. Tell your friend to become aware of the harmony in the universe and to feel the life force within. Your friend might call this life force God. The name makes no difference. Once your friend lets go of the past pain and becomes aware of the universal life force, internal healing can begin.

Ask your guardian angel for protection and help. Offer thanks to the universe for allowing you to help your friend in this way. Feel your guardian angel around you, and then, when you feel ready, count from one to five and open your eyes.

You can also send healing energies to entire groups of people. Ministers frequently hold prayers for the sick and suffering during church services. You can do the same in your own home. Imagine hospital wards filled with healing angels, all doing their best to help the patients get well again. You can achieve this through your own prayers.

You need not kneel down and close your eyes to achieve this, either. If you have no religious background, this will not be appropriate, anyway. Simply visualize angels coming down to assist the healing process wherever you wish.

You might be driving past a hospital, for instance. As you go by, visualize the angels coming down and sitting on the end of each bed to offer help, comfort, and healing energies. Imagine the amount of good that would be achieved if just a handful of people did that every day.

An acquaintance of mine was nine years old when she saw angels for the first time. "We were enjoying a family picnic in a park," she recalls. "Below us was a large hospital. My father mentioned that a friend of his was in there waiting for a heart operation. As I looked at the hospital, I saw thousands of angels descending and passing through the roof. I told my father that his friend would be all right. He said that was unlikely, as his friend was seriously ill and not expected to survive. But I was right. His friend made a complete recovery and surprised everyone.

"Several months later, this man came to our house for dinner and asked me how I knew he would survive. Up until then I had spoken to no one about the angels, but I told this man what I had seen. He hugged me when I told him that, because he had seen an angel standing beside his bed. Since then I have seen angels several times, and I never go past a hospital without remembering that family picnic."

Angels have been seen in a wide range of healing places. Charles Leadbeater recorded a service of healing that he gave at the Liberal Catholic Church when a large angel appeared and gave healing to the seventy-nine patients present. His report in *The Theosophist* said all the patients "felt much better, at any rate for the time, and with some of them the improvement seems to last, while with others it slowly passes away. The most striking thing is the wonderful spiritual outpouring that they all feel."[1] In the same report, Leadbeater wrote that this angel worked "hard and incessantly" at the church, but was also healing in at least thirty other places at the same time.

A ministry of healing angels was first referred to in the Book of Tobit, one of the books in the Apocrypha.[2] In this book Tobit tells how Raphael provided a formula for healing. The story is fascinating.

Tobit was a good, upright, honest, pious Jew, who was exiled in Nineveh some eight hundred years before the birth of Christ. The Jewish people had been taken captive in Nineveh and King Sennacherib would not allow them to bury their dead. However, Tobit and a handful of other brave people defied the king and secretly buried the corpses.

One evening, when Tobit was fifty years old, he was sitting down to enjoy his dinner when he heard of another body that needed to be buried. He immediately went and buried it. As he had been defiled from handling the body he did not bother to return home, but slept by the wall of a courtyard. Unfortunately, he left his face uncovered.

During the night, the droppings of sparrows who were resting on the wall fell into his eyes, and when he woke up he was totally blind. He did everything possible to regain his sight, but even the best physicians were unable to help. His wife was forced to work so the family could survive.

Eight years later, Tobit was suicidal and called on God, pleading with him to let him die. He started to get his affairs in order, and asked Tobias, his only son, to travel to Media to collect some money that he was owed by a business associate there. He told Tobias to find someone to travel with him for safety, and said he would pay the man for his time and work.

At the same time this was happening in Nineveh, a woman named Sarah was also suffering in Media. She had been possessed by a demon named Asmodeus,[3] who had killed all seven men she had married before the marriages could be consummated. Her parents were worried that they would never find a husband for their daughter. Her father, Raguel, prayed to God for help.

When God heard the prayers of both Tobit and Raguel, he sent Raphael down to earth to restore Tobit's sight and exorcise the demon from Sarah.

Tobias found someone to go with him to Media: this was actually Raphael in human form. He told Tobias that his name was Azarias, and that he was distantly related to Tobit.

Tobias and Raphael left for Media. When Tobias washed himself in the Tigris River on the first night, a huge fish appeared and looked as if it would swallow him whole. Raphael told him to catch it, which Tobias managed to do. When it was on the bank Raphael told him to cut out the fish's heart, liver, and gall. They cooked and ate the rest of the fish.

When Tobias asked Azarias (Raphael) why they had saved the heart, liver, and gall, he was told that a smoke made from the heart and liver would exorcise evil spirits, while the gall would restore the sight of a man with a white film in his eyes.

The pair continued on the journey. When they got close to Media, Raphael told Tobias that they should stay in the house of Raguel, and that he should marry Raguel's daughter, Sarah. Not surprisingly, Tobias became concerned when he learned that all seven of her previous husbands had died on their wedding nights. Raphael reassured him, telling him that on his wedding night he should place some of the heart and liver from the fish on incense to create smoke. The demon would leave Sarah as soon as he smelled the smoke, and never return.

It all happened as Raphael had promised. The demon Asmodeus fled as soon as he smelled the smoke and was "banished to upper Egypt," where Raphael tied him up.

The wedding celebrations lasted for fourteen days, and then Tobias took his bride, Sarah, and Raphael back home to Nineveh. Tobias anointed his father's eyes with the gall of the fish, and Tobit's sight was miraculously restored. The family was delighted and offered Raphael half of the money that Tobias had brought back from Media.

Raphael then revealed himself as the archangel he really was. Tobit and Tobias fell to the ground in terror, but Raphael told them not to be afraid. He told the men that he was one of the seven angels who were closest to God, and that he had taken Tobit's prayers directly to God. He exhorted the men to lead good, righteous lives, to praise God, and to write down everything that had happened.

Raphael continues his healing ministry to this day.

Healing Yourself

There are many types of healing and it is to our advantage to ask our guardian angels for help whenever we need it. After all, your guardian angel is there to help, guide, and protect you all the way through your life. It seems foolish not to ask for help when you need it. Yet many people are reluctant to ask. They adopt a "stiff upper lip" attitude and suffer unnecessarily.

Your guardian angel can help when you are physically ill, and is also only too pleased to help when you are mentally, emotionally, or spiritually unwell. There are times when we all need healing in these different areas.

Several months ago a friend of mine experienced a mental breakdown. It had been building up for years, his wife told me, but when it happened it was still a shock for the family. Grant had been working extremely long hours, trying to keep the division of the corporation he worked for afloat. It had been an uphill battle, as a third of his staff had been laid off, and others were leaving all the time as they found more secure positions. Eventually, it all became too much.

One night, Grant failed to come home from work. His son drove to his office to see if he was ignoring the phone, and found he had left at his normal time. The police were contacted, and Grant was found the next morning sitting on a park bench, almost dead from the cold.

"Someone was looking after him," his doctor said. "By rights, he should have frozen to death."

Over the long months of recovery, Grant repeatedly saw angels. They terrified him to begin with, but he gradually came to see them as healing angels. For the first time in his life he began thinking about spiritual matters. He is not yet back at work, but his family cannot believe the changes in him.

"He's rejoined the human race," his wife says. "He's tolerant, understanding and loving. He no longer gets impatient with the children, and he's discovered what's really important in life."

He has also discovered, and is in regular communication with, his guardian angel.

A lady I know experienced emotional healing with the help of her guardian angel. I will call her Carol, though that is not her real name, as she is still very embarrassed about what she did.

Several years ago, when Carol was thirty, she fell in love with a man named Howard, twenty years older. Every day, she bought a newspaper from a kiosk on her way to work, and gradually became infatuated with Howard, the owner of the stand.

Finally he invited her out for dinner. The relationship progressed and soon she moved into his apartment. Everything went well for a while, but Howard gradually came to resent the different ways in which she tried to change him. One night they had a major argument and the next day she moved out.

That should have been the end of the relationship. In fact, it was as far as Howard was concerned. However, Carol brooded about the relationship endlessly. She began spying on Howard to see if he was seeing other women. She watched him at work, also, to see if he gave the women customers more attention than the men. She began going through his trash to see if there was any evidence of a woman living with him. She became totally obsessed.

One day she called in to work and said she was sick. She went across town to Howard's apartment and broke in. She was still searching Howard's home when he came back unexpectedly. A neighbor had phoned him to tell him that a woman had climbed in through his bathroom window. Howard had not called the police, as he knew who it would be.

Carol broke down in his arms, apologized, and pleaded to be allowed back. As gently as he could, Howard told her that this was impossible.

On her way home Carol was involved in an accident. To this day she does not know if she was trying to commit suicide, but the accident was entirely her fault. She spent a week in a hospital. During her recovery she wrote Howard several letters every day professing her love for him.

One morning she walked to the post office with several letters for Howard. As she walked, she heard a persistent voice.

"Why do you never listen to me?" she heard, repeated again and again. She looked around, but saw nothing.

"Are you talking to me?" she said out loud.

"Go back home," the voice told her. "I want to talk to you."

"I'll just post these letters first," Carol said.

"No, no, no!" the voice said in exasperation. "Go home now!"

The voice was so strong and insistent, Carol told me later, that she obeyed. She returned home, made some coffee and sat outside in the sun to see what would happen.

As she sat there, trying to understand where the voice had come from, she became aware that she was not alone. She could not see anyone, but there was a comforting presence beside her.

"It was weird," she said. "I was interested in psychic things, and I also read my daily horoscope, but angels?" She shook her head. "No way!" She smiled at the memory. "Anyway, somehow it dawned on me that it was an angel. I had vague memories of a friend telling me about her guardian angel years ago, but I wasn't interested then, and hadn't paid much attention. Now, here I was, with an angel right beside me!"

The angel was in no hurry to talk, and allowed Carol plenty of time to become familiar with the situation before starting. The angel did not speak out loud, but allowed the words to flow into Carol's mind. Carol felt as if scales had been taken off her eyes.

"I could suddenly see what a fool I'd made of myself. I felt so ashamed and embarrassed, but my angel told me to forget that, to just let it go. I could almost see all the hurt and pain leaving me and floating away. I felt so much peace and warmth and love flowing from that angel. I just sat there, bathed in its presence. I must have fallen asleep, because it was late afternoon when I realized where I was. When I went to work the next day no one could believe the change in me, it was that obvious!"

Carol's guardian angel allowed her to heal herself emotionally. Carol wrote one final letter to Howard, apologizing and telling him that she had now managed to let him go. Several months later, when she felt brave enough to walk past his kiosk again, the sight of him meant nothing to her. She spoke briefly to him and then carried on with her day. She is now happier than ever before, and is in regular contact with her guardian angel.

Carol gave me some valuable advice about guardian angels. "All you need do," she told me, "Is open up your heart, and your guardian angel will be with you."

No matter what happens in your life, remember, you can always open up your heart and allow your guardian angel in to bathe you in healing energy.

Your guardian angel is there to help and protect you. Consequently, Harold B. Lee, the eleventh president of the Church of Jesus Christ of Latter-Day Saints, was not surprised at his experience with his guardian angel. He was flying home across the United States with a deteriorating ulcer. In the airplane he twice felt a healing hand on his head. However, when he looked up there was nothing to be seen. Shortly after arriving home, Harold Lee's ulcer started hemorrhaging. If that had happened on board the plane he would have died.[4]

The story of Saint Bernadette Soubirous and Our Lady of Lourdes, told in chapter 1, is an example of miraculous healing extended to multitudes. During Bernadette's visions of the Virgin, witnesses "already saw and treated her as if she were a saint."[5]

On February 25, 1858, Bernadette crawled on hands and knees to the back of the Massabielle grotto and scooped out some muddy water. She said that the Virgin

Mary had told her to drink and wash herself in it. Almost immediately, miraculous cures began to occur to the people who bathed in the water, and today millions of people visit Lourdes annually in the hope of being cured.

Bernadette had been asthmatic as a child and later suffered from tuberculosis. Sadly, she was never able to cure herself and was bedridden for the last few years of her short life. She died in 1879 at the age of thirty-five, and was declared a saint by the Roman Catholic Church in 1933.

6

Angels, Creativity, and the Arts

Despite the fact that I frequently meet people who claim they are not creative, I believe we all are highly creative. Every time we think a thought, we create something. If you tend a garden you are doing something creative. If you prepare a meal, you are also creating something. The problem arises because many people tend to think that creativity applies only to something artistic. I believe that we all also possess an artistic, creative side to our beings, but often have difficulty in finding it.

An elderly relative of mine did not discover that he was good at needlework until he was confined to his bed for several months. It is unlikely that he would ever have discovered this talent if he had not fallen ill.

An acquaintance of mine discovered he had a talent for playing the musical saw. Dave would never have realized this if he hadn't spent a summer vacation living outdoors and cutting down trees. One night, a friend told him that he had seen someone playing a saw, and Dave immediately decided to try it on one of the saws they had been using. To his amazement, he was able to create music on it.

A relative survived a particularly difficult time in her life by writing down all her pent-up emotions. She is now making money from her short stories.

All of these people discovered their talents by accident. Of course, some people know, virtually from the day they were born, what their special talents are. Mozart is a perfect example. He was playing the harpsichord and composing music at the age of four.

Most of us are not that fortunate, and some people go through their entire lives never finding out what their talents are. There is no need for that to happen. All we need do is ask our guardian angels for help in finding our talents. Our guardian angels will also help us to develop our talents once we've found them.

Poets and artists of all sorts regularly include angels in their works. In a way, this is not surprising, as poets and artists deal with emotions and feelings at the very deepest levels. Origen, the famous early theologian, believed that angels were involved in the creation of language, so they have been involved with words from the very beginning of time.[1]

William Blake (1757–1827) was a visionary and mystic as well as a romantic rebel. He was influenced by the works of Emanuel Swedenborg and frequently included angels in his poems and drawings. At the age of nine, he saw angels for the first time during a solitary walk in the country. He came home and told his parents that he had seen "a tree full of angels."[2] Obviously, angels were around him all the time as he was creating. In fact, in the preface to *A New Jerusalem* he said that the poem had been dictated to him and all he did was write it down. "I am not ashamed," he wrote, "to tell you what ought to be told—that I am under the direction of messengers from heaven, daily and nightly."[3] In fact, William Blake immersed himself so much into his visionary world that his wife said: "I have very little of Mr. Blake's company. He is always in Paradise."[4]

I have always loved William Blake's poem "Holy Thursday" from his *Songs of Innocence*:

'Twas on a Holy Thursday, their innocent faces clean,
Came children walking two and two, in red, and blue,
and green;
Gray-headed beadles walked before, with wands as
white as snow,
Till into the high dome of Paul's they like Thames
waters flow.
O what a multitude they seemed, these flowers of
London town!

Seated in companies they sit, with radiance all their own;
The hum of multitudes was there, but multitudes of lambs,
Thousands of little boys and girls raising their innocent hands.

Now, like a mighty wind, they raise to heaven the voice of song,
Or like harmonious thunderings the seats of heaven among;
Beneath them sit the agèd men, wise guardians of the poor,
Then cherish pity, lest you drive an angel from your door.

Francis Thompson (1859–1907) was a mystic, like Blake. As a child I loved hearing his poem "Little Jesus:"

Little Jesus, wast thou shy
Once, and just so small as I?
And what did it feel like to be
Out of heaven, and just like me?
Didst Thou sometimes think of there,
And ask where all the angels were?

I should think that I would cry
For my house all made of sky;
I would look about the air,
And wonder where my angels were;
And at waking 'twould distress me—
Not an angel there to dress me!

Hadst Thou ever any toys,
Like us little girls and boys?
And didst Thou play in heaven with all
The angels, that were not too tall

With stars for marbles? Did the things
Play Can you see me? *through their wings?*

My mother used to enjoy reading poems by the "poet of childhood," Eugene Field (1850–1895). When I was a child his poem "Little Boy Blue" always brought me to tears.

The little toy dog is covered with dust,
But sturdy and stanch he stands;
And the little toy soldier is red with rust,
And his musket moulds in his hands.
Time was when the little toy dog was new,
And the soldier was passing fair;
And that was the time when our Little Boy Blue
Kissed them and put them there.

"Now, don't you go till I come," he said,
"And don't you make any noise!"
So, toddling off to his trundle-bed,
He dreamt of the pretty toys;
And, as he was dreaming, an angel song
Awakened our Little Boy Blue—
Oh! the years are many, the years are long,
But the little toy friends are true!

Aye, faithful to Little Boy Blue they stand,
Each in the same old place—
Awaiting the touch of a little hand,
The smile of a little face;
And they wonder, as waiting the long years through
In the dust of that little chair,
What has become of our Little Boy Blue,
Since he kissed them and put them there.

My other main angel memory from childhood is reciting the prayer quoted in *A Candle in the Dark* by Thomas Ady (c. 1655). It is not known whether Ady wrote this prayer.

Matthew, Mark, Luke and John,
The Bed be blest that I lie on,
Four angels to my bed,
Four angels round my head,
One to watch, and one to pray,
And two to bear my soul away.

Leigh Hunt (1784–1859) wrote his famous poem "Abou Ben Adhem" after being influenced by Islamic ideas about angels. Moslems believe that we have two angels guarding us during the day, and another two at night. These angels also write down everything we do for judgment day.

Abou Ben Adhem (may his tribe increase!)
Awoke one night from a deep dream of peace,
And saw within the moonlight in his room,
Making it rich, and like a lily in bloom,
An Angel, writing in a book of gold;
Exceeding peace had made Ben Adhem bold,
And to the presence in the room he said,
"What writest thou?"—The vision raised its head,
And with a look made of all sweet accord,
Answer'd, "The names of those who love the Lord."
"And is mine one?" said Abou. "Nay, not so,"
Replied the angel. Abou spoke more low,
But cheerily still; and said, "I pray thee, then,
Write me as one that loves his fellowmen."
The angel wrote and vanish'd. The next night

It came again, with a great wakening light,
And show'd the names whom love of God had bless'd,
And, lo! Ben Adhem's name led all the rest.

Robert Browning (1812–1889) was happy to give the credit for his poetic genius to angels. In "Pauline" he wrote:

And of my powers, one springs up to save
From utter death a soul with such desire
Confined to clay—of powers the only one
That marks me—an imagination which
Has been a very angel, coming not
In fitful visions, but beside me ever
And never failing me.

Whenever I read "Pauline," I'm reminded of the famous remark of Michelangelo: "In that rough black rock, my friends, I see an angel. And I mean to set him free."

Many poets have seen angels, but one of the most startling examples inspired William Cowper (1731–1800) to compose "God Moves in Mysterious Ways His Wonders to Perform." Cowper suffered from depression for most of his life, and in his twenties spent eighteen months in an asylum after a suicide attempt. In 1799, after some years of dark despair, Cowper hailed a horse-drawn cab and asked the driver to take him to the Thames River, where he intended to drown himself. It was a foggy evening and the driver drove around aimlessly until he was completely lost. He told Cowper that he could not even take him back home. Cowper got out of the cab and found that he was right outside his home. Cowper thought the cab driver must have been an angel in disguise.

Fra Angelico (c.1400–1455), the famous Renaissance artist, saw angels in his bedroom every morning when he woke, and he was able to include them in his paintings.

The golden age of angels in art ended in the fifteenth century. In this period the writings of Pseudo-Dionysius were being challenged; two popes, each claiming infallibility, were trying to lead their respective flocks, and the Black Death had reduced the population of Europe by half. Theologians were arguing that Jesus Christ could stand on his own, without the need of choirs of angels. After the plague the general population had good reason to wonder why the healing, ministering angels had not come to their assistance when they most needed it. Consequently, angels began to diminish in importance.

In the sixteenth and seventeenth centuries, angels were dealt another blow when science discovered the laws and forces of nature, proving that it was not angels who moved the stars and controlled gravity.

However, angels did not die out completely, and remained in popular art and music. It is said that, even today, one in every ten popular songs mentions angels.[5]

Composers throughout the ages have also been greatly influenced by angels. Countless congregations sing hymns with words praising angels. "Sing, choirs of angels" and "Hark! The herald angels sing" are just two lines that come to mind.

George Frideric Handel (1685–1759) composed *The Messiah*, his most famous oratorio, in just twenty-four days. His servant came into the room just after Handel had completed the "Hallelujah Chorus" and found him crying with joy and excitement. When he was asked how he felt as he composed the famous chorus, Handel replied: "I did think I saw all Heaven before me and the great God Himself."[6]

The stage has also received its share of angelic attention. In *Alfred: A Masque*, James Thomson (1700–1748) managed to combine guardian angels and patriotism:

When Britain first, at Heaven's command,
Arose from out the azure main,
This was the charter of the land,
And guardian angels sung this strain:
"Rule, Britannia, rule the waves;
Britons never will be slaves."

William Shakespeare (1564–1616) frequently mentioned angels in his plays and sonnets. In *Hamlet* (1.iv.39), for instance, he wrote: "Angels and ministers of grace defend us!" In the next act (2.ii.303), Hamlet's famous speech includes the words:

What a piece of work is a man! How noble in reason! how infinite in faculty! in form and moving how express and admirable! in action, how like an angel! in apprehension how like a god! the beauty of the world! the paragon of animals! And yet, to me, what is this quintessence of dust? Man delights not me—no, nor woman neither...

Shakespeare includes a wonderful good-night in this play, when Horatio says to Hamlet (5.ii.351): "Good night, sweet prince, And flights of angels sing thee to thy rest!"

In *The Merchant of Venice* (5.i.54), Lorenzo says:

Look how the floor of heaven
Is thick inlaid with patines of bright gold;
There's not the smallest orb which thou behold'st
But in his motion like an angel sings,
Still quiring to the young-ey'd cherubins,
Such harmony is in immortal souls,
But whilst this muddy vesture of decay
Doth grossly close it in, we cannot hear it.

Shakespeare has Isabella, in *Measure for Measure*, make a highly perceptive comment (2.ii.117):

But man, proud man,
Dress'd in a little brief authority,
Most ignorant of what he's most assur'd,
His glassy essence, like an angry ape,
Plays such fantastic tricks before high heaven
As makes the angels weep.

All the people I have mentioned here, and countless millions more, have evoked angels in imagery or called on angelic assistance to enhance their creativity. Next time you want to write a letter, bake a cake, plant something in the garden, or do anything that you consider in any way creative, call on your guardian angel for assistance. It will be given willingly, and you will be amazed to discover how creative you really are.

7

Your Angel Diary

Every request I have ever made to my guardian angel has been acted upon, but often not in the way I expected. Occasionally, I have been disappointed with what I considered an inexplicable lack of success. However, further investigation has always shown that my request had been answered in the best possible way for everyone concerned.

For instance, several years ago I seriously considered moving to another country. It seemed sensible and logical at the time, as I felt stifled where I was, and great opportunities beckoned from overseas.

Naturally, the move would have meant a great upheaval for my family, but I thought the benefits would ultimately outweigh the temporary difficulties. I asked my guardian angel for guidance, and waited, confident that I would be encouraged to move.

To my surprise, the response was negative and my guardian angel told me to look around where I was. This was not the advice I wanted, and I asked again for guidance, this time clearly pointing out all the advantages I could see in emigrating.

While I was waiting for a response, I was offered a valuable opportunity less than five miles from home. Further opportunities came my way, almost without effort, and I soon found myself busier than I'd ever been before.

It took me some time to realize that this was my guardian angel's work. My guardian angel was aware that I felt hemmed in and restricted where I was and was looking overseas for fresh opportunities, so provided me with more opportunities than I could handle in my own backyard!

Even though our guardian angels sometimes work in mysterious ways, they always have our best interests at heart. I have no idea what would have happened if I had uprooted the family and transported them halfway around the world. Perhaps it would have worked out well, but it may also have been a disaster. My guardian angel resolved the situation for me in the best possible way, even though it was not the answer I wanted to hear at the time.

For some years I have kept an angel diary to record my contacts with the angelic kingdom. This allows me to go back and see how different situations have been handled and resolved. You will find it very useful to do the same. It does not need to be an elaborate journal that you fill in laboriously every day. I may go a week or more without writing anything in my diary, but every time something concerning angels occurs I jot down a few notes.

An angel diary will provide absolute proof that your guardian angel—and, in fact, the entire angelic kingdom—is looking after you and working in your best interests. In a matter of months you will have a fascinating series of accounts of your personal angel experiences. You will be able to see how your personal requests have been handled, and you will have gained total confidence in your guardian angel.

A Record of Change

Not long ago I was talking with a young woman named Sharleen, who had just completed a bachelor's degree.

"What are you going to do now?" I asked.

"I'm planning a trip to India," she replied. "I'll be working there as a volunteer at a Christian mission for two years."

This was not what I had expected to hear. I had assumed that Sharleen would enter the work force, or return to college to gain more qualifications. The story she told me was fascinating.

Sharleen started keeping a diary at the age of fifteen. At the age of seventeen she dropped out of high school and ran away from home with her boyfriend. The adventure was disastrous, but she learned a great deal from it. She and her boyfriend had to work extremely hard at low-paying jobs to afford the rent and food. They discovered that life at a subsistence level was no fun. Sharleen recorded all of this in her diary.

Sharleen began having strange dreams. Every night an angel appeared, telling her to return home and go back to school. She tried to ignore this advice. She tried going to bed later, but the angel still appeared in her dreams. Not even alcohol and drugs could stop the angel from appearing.

"He was so good and patient," Sharleen said. "He never got mad at me. He just kept insisting that I contact my parents and go home. In my dreams I swore and yelled, but he simply stood there, calm and serene. He was so infuriating!"

The angel told Sharleen to call him "Zymar." She was never sure if he was male or female, and Zymar always dismissed questions about that as unimportant.

"I call Zymar a male, as he is so strong and masterful," she said. "But he has the most gorgeous, beautiful face and long flowing hair. I'd love to look like that!"

After a while, Zymar started appearing in the daytime as well. "I was working in this burger bar," she said. "It was lunchtime and I had a long line of people to serve. I looked up for the next person and there was my angel smiling at me." Sharleen grinned at the memory. "I freaked out! It was bad enough having him in my dreams, but I didn't want him turning up at work as well. I screamed at him to go, and as I did, he sort of faded away and I found myself yelling at the next customer. I came close to losing my job that day."

Zymar kept appearing. One evening she was walking home from work and felt him by her side. She couldn't see him, but she knew he was there.

"It was comforting," Sharleen said. "Scary, but comforting at the same time. I was pleased in one way that he wasn't visible, as I didn't want other people to see me walking home with an angel beside me. But he kept talking. Not out loud. The words just flowed into my mind. All the usual things about going home and getting an education. I knew he was right. I'd always known he was right, but I didn't want to hear it.

"I started running to get away from him, but he kept up easily. When I got home I slammed the door shut and he seemed to stay outside. Malcolm wasn't home, so I wrote it all down in my diary and that made me feel better. When I'd finished I flipped back a few pages and found that almost all the entries were about this angel. I couldn't remember writing any of it down, but it was all there in my handwriting. I read it over and over again.

"I think Malcolm was working at a packaging factory at the time, moving big pallets of cardboard around. He was always tired and grumpy. He got home about nine and I hadn't got supper ready. We had an argument and went to bed hungry. The next day I went back home."

Life at home was no easier. Zymar kept visiting her, even appearing in class. One day he asked her what she wanted to do with her life.

"I had no idea. I just wanted to have fun. You should have seen the look on Zymar's face when I told him that!"

Over the next few months Zymar kept telling Sharleen to continue with her education. "I had no idea how often he pushed that thought into my mind," Sharleen said, "until I looked at my diary. It was every day, sometimes two or three times a day—and it went on for months!"

Sharleen tried to ignore Zymar's suggestions.

"Eventually, it started to make sense. Malcolm and I had tried to live on minimum wages. I didn't want to spend the rest of my life doing that. I started to pay more attention to my schoolwork. My friends noticed right away and teased me about it, but I didn't care. My angel was always there to keep me motivated and on track. My grades improved and I graduated second in my class. No one, especially my parents, could believe it.

"I did the same at college. With Zymar by my side I could do no wrong. I was motivated and worked hard. One day I realized that I was happier than I'd ever been in my whole life. And it was all thanks to my guardian angel. Yes, it took me a long time to realize just who he was. He's stayed with me all the time. I'd probably still be serving burgers if it hadn't been for Zymar!"

Halfway through her last year at college her guardian angel steered her into a section of the university library that she had not been in before.

"There were all these books about children in Africa and India. One book seemed to jump out of the shelves at me. I took it home and read it. Then I came back and read virtually all the others. Zymar would usually sit and read along with me.

"I was thinking about my future, whether to go out in the work force or carry on and get a doctorate. Zymar suggested I work in India for a while. Everyone was shocked when I told them about it, but I'm sure it's the right thing to do. My angel thinks so. I was going back through my diary last night and couldn't believe how many references there were to India going back years and years. I think Zymar knew well before I did that I was going to do this thing."

"What will you do when you do come back?" I asked.

Sharleen grinned. "I don't know yet, but I'm sure my guardian angel does!"

Sharleen had found her diary invaluable in many ways, particularly as it gave her such a clear picture of her relationship and dealings with her guardian angel. It also allowed her to go back and see exactly how situations had occurred, developed, and been resolved. She was constantly amazed at how references had come up months, and even years, before they became manifest in her own life.

Sharleen had begun keeping a diary two years before meeting her guardian angel and enjoyed writing down her feelings and experiences. Even if you do not enjoy writing, you will find it helpful to jot down a few key words every now and again. You will probably find that your entries grow longer as your relationship with your guardian angel develops.

One of the most important parts of keeping a diary is to keep a record of your requests and to evaluate the results. I find that often I forget what I have asked for and my diary enables me to keep track of this as well. Your diary also allows you to keep a record of your growth and insights, and will help you to measure your progress. It will become more and more valuable as time goes by because you will be able to discern a pattern that provides a graphic account of your development.

Once you start an angel diary you will find yourself looking for things to record in it. It will gain more and more importance in your life, and gradually give you a clear sense of what you want out of life and where you are going.

8

Your Angel Altar

An angel altar creates a special place in your home where you can instantly be in tune with your guardian angel. I discovered this quite accidentally. I had spent a wonderful day in the Yorkshire Moors of England and had visited Fountains Abbey. Although the abbey is in ruins today, it is still an extremely holy and spiritual place. That evening I commented to my host that a large number of the places I had been to contained so much spiritual energy that it was impossible not to sense it.

My friend agreed and told me that the next day I would visit a place where the spiritual energy superseded anything I had experienced yet. He would say no more, and I was forced to wait until the following day.

The next morning we explored Harrogate and visited some second-hand bookstores. I love the energy these places put out, but it could not be described as spiritual, in the sense that my friend and I meant. In the evening we went to have dinner with my friend's cousin, Sarah.

As soon as I walked into her home I could feel the energy all around me. It was an astonishing, enveloping feeling that was comforting, soothing and spiritual. I looked around the living room for some sign as to where all this energy was coming from. When Sarah left the room to check on the dinner, I got up and walked around. The energy seemed to be coming from a small side table that stood against one wall, next to a grandfather clock.

The energy was definitely spiritual, but there seemed to be nothing special about the table. It was made of mahogany and was obviously very old. On top were several framed photographs, including one of the friend I was staying with.

I was still standing in front of this table when our hostess returned. Sarah stood in the doorway, a half-smile on her face, waiting for me to say something.

"This table," I said. "There's something spiritual about it. I could feel it as soon as I walked in. What is it?"

Sarah beamed. "I'm glad you can feel it," she said. "It's what keeps me going. That's my angel altar."

Over dinner she told me all about her altar.

"It started as a place where I could call on my guardian angel," she explained. "It was not originally an altar. I just wanted somewhere in the house where I could feel especially close to my guardian angel, and I also wanted a place for her. It's worked out better than I ever thought it would."

Sarah began by placing a Bible on the table, thinking that this would make the table and immediate surroundings more spiritual.

"But it didn't work," she told us. "It only began working when I put a few of my most valued possessions on it. After a week or two, I changed them to see what would happen. Then I tried crystals, and finally I put my precious photographs on it. For some reason, that really made things hum. My altar has transformed the whole house. It used to be gloomy and sort of sad, but now it's vibrant and happy. The house seems to have moved from permanent winter into perpetual summer."

"Do you pray at your altar?" I asked.

"Sometimes, I guess. I tend to pray all the time, in a way. I carry on this inner conversation everywhere I go, so I guess you could say I'm praying all the time."

"To God?"

Sarah nodded. "Of course. Maybe I don't see him quite the way you do, but I have a clear picture of him in my own mind."

"How do you contact your guardian angel at your altar?"

"That's easy." Sarah smiled. "She comes whenever I want, but I always feel so close to her when I'm by the altar.

I sit down in that chair over there, and immediately start talking, and my angel responds."

"What else do you do with your altar?"

"Everything that comes in or goes out of the house stops at my altar for a second or two. Even the groceries." Sarah held up her wine glass. "Even the wine we're drinking tonight." She held up a hand to stop me from asking a question. "I believe that putting things on my altar blesses them. If I have a gift for someone, I always rest it on my altar for a while after I've wrapped it. That gives the present so much more power and energy. I do the same when someone buys me something. It goes straight on my altar and gets charged with angel energy."

"What do the photographs do?"

Sarah shrugged. "I think it must be because they're photos of people I love. Those feelings of love must make it a special spot for my angel."

"Tell him about your library books," my friend said.

Sarah laughed. "Yes, I confess. I even put my library books on the altar for a while before reading them. I think it does them good, and it seems to revitalize them before I start reading." She shook her head. "Now you'll think I'm really weird!"

"Not at all," I said. "The first thing I'll do when I get home is set up an altar."

You can also benefit from setting up your own altar. It can be anywhere you wish, but I feel that the best results come if it is placed in a room that is used every day. Because it need not look like a church altar, you can place it anywhere, and people who are not interested will not notice it.

It makes no difference how large or small it is. Sarah had a special table, which is a good idea. If you cannot do that, use a shelf or part of a dressing table.

Once you have decided on the right position, and your angel guardian will provide advice on this if you ask, you must determine to use this spot only as an altar. You must never use it simply as a place to deposit items. It must be treated with respect.

Experiment with different objects to see which create the most energy. I have a few crystals as well as photographs on my altar. You might like to try keeping fresh flowers on your altar as well. Someone I used to know keeps a small wooden box on her altar and this is full of precious objects from her childhood. None of them have any value at all, except to her. Because she loves them all, they are perfect on her altar.

A friend of mine who is a practicing Christian has a Bible, a prayer book, and a framed picture of Jesus on her altar. Behind it she has placed a shepherd's staff. She finds that these are all helpful for her.

Your altar can be anywhere at all. You may prefer to have it out of doors, particularly if you have a favorite place where you are unlikely to be disturbed. Beside a stream, under a tree, or in an open meadow might be an ideal place for you.

You may find that inside a church is the right place for you. Naturally, you would not be able to leave any special items there, and you would be able to visit only when the church was open. The church may be of any denomination, and it need not be one that you normally attend. The important thing is that it feels right for you.

If you set up your altar inside your house, you will quickly notice a change in the energy in the room. You will feel a sense of calmness and peace whenever you go near. You will also find that you can speak freely and easily to your guardian angel when you are close to your altar. Naturally, you will be able to summon your angel any time you wish, but you will find the contact to be immediate when you use your altar.

Your altar can also be used for healing. You will find that after you have had your altar for a while, and have used it regularly, that both the quality and quantity of sacred energy that is produced will increase. You can mentally transmit this spiritual, healing energy wherever you wish. Whenever you hear of someone who could benefit from this energy, you can mentally send some to them. You can be as generous with it as you like, as it is produced at such a rate that it can never run out.

A friend of mine has been deeply involved in spiritual development for a long time, but his wife is an atheist. Consequently, this passion of his is never discussed in the home. All the same, he has an angel altar in his living room, which he uses all the time. Not long ago his wife commented on the beautiful feelings she received whenever she was in the living room. It shows that the powerful energies emanating from an angel altar can be experienced by everyone, even professed atheists.

Your altar can be used for self-development, for healing and for spreading love, compassion and understanding. It can also be used for forgiveness.

We all feel hurt at times by the things that other people say and do. If someone hurts you, either accidentally or intentionally, practice sending forgiveness to that person from your angel altar. The results will far surpass your expectations. There is enormous healing value in forgiving others. It will feel as if a large weight has been taken away from you. You will also find yourself becoming more tolerant and accepting of others. We need to accept and love people for what they are, not for what we would like them to be. By accepting others as they are, life becomes smoother, easier, and much happier.

By setting up an angel altar and using it regularly, your relationship with your guardian angel, and the entire angelic kingdom, will become closer than ever before. You probably know what it feels like to have a special close friend with whom you can freely discuss anything at all. If you use your angel altar, your relationship with your guardian angel will be thousands of times better than that.

Your angel altar can transform your life.

9

Gemstones and Your Guardian Angel

An extremely effective way of carrying your guardian angel with you everywhere you go is to charge a crystal or gemstone with your guardian angel's energy. Virtually any gemstone will do for this, so if you have a gemstone that is important to you for some reason, use it. Perhaps a friend gave you a gemstone or crystal that you particularly like, or maybe you bought one simply because it seemed special. These crystals and gemstones are ideal.

If you do not already have a gemstone that is important to you in this way, or perhaps want a gemstone dedicated solely to your guardian angel, there are a number of ways of finding one.

You may find visiting a crystal shop or a New Age bookstore provides a crystal or gemstone that draws itself to you. I have frequently gone into stores that sell crystals with no intention of buying anything, but found that a particular gemstone chose me. When this happens I always buy it, because I know there is a reason for the attraction, even if it is not apparent at the time.

You may find that once you think about buying a gemstone, someone will suddenly give you one. This is simply the universe working. I am always delighted when something serendipitous like that happens.

Many years ago, when I was living in London, I was searching for a particular out-of-print book. I couldn't find a copy anywhere, and was on my way to place an advertisement for a copy in a book collectors' magazine. I walked out of the Underground and bumped into a friend on the escalator. While we had a cup of coffee together he enthusiastically told me about a book he had just finished reading, and offered to lend it to me. It was the same book that I was on my way to advertise for!

You might find it worth telling friends that you are looking for a suitable crystal or gemstone. One of them may wish to give you one as an early Christmas or birthday present.

If none of the above works, you can choose one by using either numerology or astrology. You will recall learning your Life Path Number in chapter 4. Each number relates not only to a color, but also to a variety of stones.

Life Path Numbers

1 Onyx, hematite, red jasper, turquoise.

2 Agate, emerald, pearl.

3 Zircon, topaz, turquoise.

4 Beryl, coral, sapphire.

5 Variegated agate, topaz, amethyst.

6 Agate, amber, emerald.

7 Bloodstone, red garnet, obsidian.

8 Diamond, jet, onyx.

9 Amber, coral, moonstone, pearl.

11 Amethyst, bloodstone, garnet.

22 Amethyst, coral, diamond.

Day of the Month (Birth Date)

1 (1st, 10th, 19th, and 28th): Amber, ruby, topaz.

2 (2nd, 11th, 20th, and 29th): Jade, moonstone, pearl.

3 (3rd, 12th, 21st, and 30th): Amethyst, turquoise.

4 (4th, 13th, 22nd, and 31st): Sapphire and topaz.

5 (5th, 14th, and 23rd): Diamond, sapphire.

6 (6th, 15th, and 24th): Emeralds, turquoise.

7 (7th, 16th, and 25th): Cat's eye, green jade, moonstone, pearl.

8 (8th, 17th, and 26th): Diamond, black pearls.

9 (9th, 18th, and 27th): Bloodstone, garnet, ruby.

With astrology you have even more choices, as you can choose a stone from your zodiac sign, the ruling planet of that sign, or one of the four elements. Take your time in choosing a stone. Usually, the stone seems to choose you, rather than the other way around.

The Zodiac Signs

Aries: Red jasper, diamond, hematite.

Taurus: Red coral, blue sapphire, emerald.

Gemini: Variegated agate.

Cancer: Amber, pearl.

Leo: Cat's eye, chrysolite, ruby.

Virgo: Beryl, peridot, sardonyx.

Libra: Agate, malachite, emerald, sapphire.

Scorpio: Amethyst, obsidian, bloodstone, opal.

Sagittarius: Blue zircon, topaz, turquoise.

Capricorn: Jet, onyx, turquoise.

Aquarius: Amber, amethyst, blood red garnet.

Pisces: Coral, pearl, moonstone, bloodstone.

The Planets

Sun (Leo): Amber, chrysolite, topaz, zircon.

Moon (Cancer): Moonstone, gypsum, pearl, quartz crystal, fluorspar, beryl, mother-of-pearl.

Mercury (Gemini, Virgo): Opal, agate, carnelian, sardonyx, serpentine.

Venus (Taurus, Libra): Emerald, turquoise, beryl, jade, malachite.

Mars (Aries, Scorpio): Garnet, jasper, ruby, bloodstone, magnetite.

Jupiter (Sagittarius, Pisces): Amethyst, turquoise, jasper, lapis lazuli, sapphire.

Saturn (Capricorn, Aquarius): Onyx, jet, obsidian, anthracite.

Uranus (Capricorn): Topaz.

Neptune (Pisces): Rock crystal, amethyst.

Pluto (Scorpio): Diamond, topaz, moss agate, opal.

The Elements

Fire (Aries, Leo, Sagittarius): Fire opal, ruby.

Earth (Taurus, Virgo, Capricorn): Moss agate, galena, onyx.

Air (Gemini, Libra, Aquarius): Topaz, opal.

Water (Cancer, Scorpio, Pisces): Aquamarine, coral, moonstone.

Once you have your gemstone or crystal, you need to charge it. You do this by washing it in fresh rainwater and allowing it to dry naturally.

After you have done this, sit down in a quiet place with your hands facing upward in your lap, one on top of the other, with your gemstone resting on top. Make yourself as comfortable as you can, then close your eyes and go through a progressive relaxation exercise. Sitting beside your angel altar or perhaps under your oracle tree would be an ideal place to do this exercise.

When you are fully relaxed, call your guardian angel to you. Explain that you want to charge your gemstone with angelic energy and ask for your angel's help.

Within thirty seconds you should feel a response from the gemstone telling you that it is charged. When I do this, I feel a tingling sensation in the palm that is holding the gemstone. Other people tell me that for them the gemstone suddenly feels warmer, or even makes a small movement. One elderly lady I know feels no physical changes, but becomes suddenly aware with every fiber of her being that her gemstone is charged. Be aware that the response you get may not be the same as the ones that I have described here. All the same you will know, without any doubt whatsoever, when your gemstone is charged.

You can carry it wherever you go, and the built-in angel energy will travel with you. You will find it useful to hold and perhaps fondle your gemstone at different times. If you feel tired and need more energy, pick up and hold your gemstone. Hold it when you are suffering from stress, or need confidence or strength. I have even loaned my crystal to people who needed additional help to get through a difficult time.

An excellent actor I know used to suffer dreadfully from stagefright before every performance. He would be fine once he got on stage, but was a nervous wreck for hours beforehand. He now holds his angel gemstone before going on stage and finds peace and tranquility, instead of the panic and fear he used to experience.

Most of us are not placed in positions like that on a regular basis, but we can all benefit from the love, harmony, and tranquility that an angel gemstone provides.

10

Finding Your Life's Purpose with Your Guardian Angel

We are all here for a reason and purpose, even though we may not be fully aware of it. In chapter 6 we discussed using our guardian angels to help us find our talents. Our purpose in life is frequently related to our talents, but is much more important. Your life purpose is what you are here to achieve in this lifetime. For most people, the question of what you are here to do is a difficult one to answer. Wouldn't life be much easier if we knew?

We would be more clearly focused, have a ready-made goal, and feel a sense of direction. We would still need to find the motivation to achieve it, but this would not be hard once we knew what we wanted and had a plan to achieve it.

Many documented accounts of people who have had near-death experiences tell a story of profound regret when they look back at their lives from "the other side" and see that they had achieved only a fraction of what they were capable of doing. Usually, these people have become extremely motivated after recovery, because they have realized that they could—and should—be doing more with their lives than they had up until that point.

For many years I read palms in shopping malls, sometimes reading a hundred or more palms a day. Every now and again I would read the palms of people with enormous potential, and would ask them what they were doing with their lives. It would distress me to learn that most were going through life one day at a time, making no goals and with no real ambitions. All that potential was being wasted!

However, if those people knew what they were here to do, wouldn't they then go out and do it? Of course, some wouldn't, but many would.

Many years ago I knew a woman who was a talented artist, singer, and writer. She was also extremely attractive and worked for a while as a model. She had the ability to make her mark in any of these fields, but has achieved absolutely nothing with her life.

There are many reasons for this. Lack of confidence and insecurity certainly played a part. I think fear may have been involved as well. However, the main causes of this woman's downfall were drugs and alcohol. She has spent most of her adult life in a haze. She still talks about all the great things she is going to achieve, but unless she changes her lifestyle drastically, she will end up living a wasted life. It is particularly sad when you think about all the gifts and opportunities she had.

Contrast her with someone such as Helen Keller (1880–1968), who lived a life of extraordinary accomplishment. At the age of nineteen months she suffered an illness that left her deaf and blind, so that she could not communicate. A remarkable teacher taught Helen to read and write braille. At the age of twenty-four she graduated cum laude from Radcliffe College. She then proceeded to devote her life to helping the deaf and blind. Although she had learned to speak, she needed a translator because her speech was not easy to understand. However, this did not stop her from traveling the world lecturing and promoting social reforms. She also wrote many books about her life, beliefs, and causes.

You would expect a young child who was deaf, blind and speechless to achieve nothing, but Helen Keller achieved much, much more than most fully abled people. She knew her life's purpose, and went out into the world and achieved it.

You, too, can achieve your life's purpose and leave your mark on the world. Your purpose may well be something that you have always known, but have for some reason ignored and kept in the back of your mind.

As a child I wanted to be a writer. I had a small neighborhood newspaper that I wrote and distributed in the streets around my home. When I left school I went into book publishing, thinking that this would be a good foundation for a writing career. I then owned a bookstore, which kept me so busy that I did not even have time to think about writing. After that, my wife and I owned a number of businesses, before I became a magician and stage hypnotist. All the time I was doing these things I was thinking about writing, and every now and again, did manage to write something. However, it was not until I was in my forties that I paused and thought about what I really wanted to do. I wanted to write. For the first time in my life I was completely focused and knew where I wanted to go. Since reaching that point, I have written many books on a wide range of subjects.

The strange thing is that everyone knew what I should be doing, except for me. I went off and did all sorts of different things, because they either looked interesting or seemed to offer good financial prospects. Yet none of them was what I should have been doing to satisfy my life's purpose. When I did discover it, it was like a revelation. It had been visible, yet unseen to me, for so many years.

There is no need to wait as long as I did. I should have asked my guardian angel for help in this matter, but I became so involved in the different things I was doing that I never quite got around to it.

Start by sitting down quietly somewhere, or going for a walk, and thinking in general terms about your life. Do not make the mistake of thinking about the negative experiences. Think about the positive times and the occasions when you felt you were performing well.

Examine these times and see if there might be some way you could incorporate those positive experiences into your life's work. You might have to use lateral thinking for this. If you work full time at a fast food outlet and the greatest experiences in your life were your sporting achievements at high school, you may feel that these could not be combined. In fact, they can. To achieve those sporting successes you must have set goals and used persistence and hard work to win. You can use those qualities in any endeavor, and, if you feel your life's work is in fast foods, you will make quick progress by using them.

If this exercise does not bring anything specific to mind, ask your guardian angel.

Meditate and ask your guardian angel to make you aware of what you should be doing. Do this at least once a day for a week, and then remain patient until you get an answer. This answer may not come in the way you expect. It may come directly from your guardian angel, but it could just as easily appear as a sudden inspiration. Perhaps something a friend says may put the idea into your mind. Angels do not always work in the way we expect.

In fact, you will probably be presented with a number of ideas. Evaluate them all carefully. Take your time. Do not be concerned if it takes weeks or even months. Whatever time it takes is necessary. Even when you are not consciously thinking about the ideas, your subconscious, inner, mind will be working on them.

Once you have the right idea, pause for a while. There is no need to rush at this stage. I like to write the idea down on a piece of paper and do some brainstorming. I keep the paper in my pocket so that I can look at it every now and again. Frequently, an idea will come to me and I can write this down too. Gradually, I will become aware that this is something I really want to do. At this stage, I make plans and act on them.

Your guardian angel will not only help you find your life's purpose, but will also provide ongoing assistance. Your angel will guide and direct you, encourage you when necessary, and provide continual support.

Monica, a successful dress designer, receives constant angel guidance. She frequently asks for advice, and always stops to listen. She credits her guardian angel with every bit of success she has had.

"My angel is my creative inspiration," she says. "She also gives me emotional, physical, spiritual, and even business advice. One year I got so busy preparing for a show that I forgot everything except my work. My angel told me to slow down and take a few days off. I said that was ridiculous, and I didn't have time to get everything done, anyway. After a heated discussion I followed my angel's advice and took two days off. I drove a couple of hundred miles to get well away from work and the phone. When I got back, I found my partner had done much of the work and I had regained all my energy. We got everything done in plenty of time. We won no awards that year, but we sold all our stock!"

The key to the whole process is to ask your guardian angel for guidance, listen to that advice, and act upon it. Your guardian angel always has your best interests at heart. You should listen, no matter what the topic, and then act. That way, you and your guardian angel become an unbeatable team that can achieve anything you set your mind on.

Part Two

Spirit Guides

11

Spirit Guides

Spirit guides are people who have passed over into the next life. They have reached a high spiritual level where they are, but still retain an interest in what is going on in this world. They are not like guardian angels who protect us, but are there to help and guide us when we ask for advice.

Guides are principally concerned with our spiritual growth and are prepared to help us with it. However, as they want us to be independent and stand on our own two feet, they discourage us from asking for help every time we have a small problem.

They prefer to act as mentors, older and wiser, who have already learned the lessons we are so painfully trying to master. Communicate with your guides as often as you wish, but ask for help only when it is really necessary.

Your guides do not offer advice to you unless you ask for it. That is why some people go through their entire lives without ever realizing that they have spirit guides. Often they have not even heard of them, let alone learned how to ask their guides for help. However, even in these cases, their spirit guides will do all they can to help these people as they travel through life. In fact, if a person like this is in desperate straits, and calls out for help from whoever he or she calls God, help will come immediately from the person's spirit guides.

Spirit guides are totally non-judgmental. Even if we make serious mistakes by ignoring or going against their advice they will be ready and willing to help again next time. They will never say, "I told you so." They recognize that we have to make mistakes sometimes to learn important lessons.

Your spirit guides will become your best friends if you allow them to be. They are concerned, caring, loving, and supportive, and have your best interests at heart all the time. But first you have to allow them into your life.

We all have spirit guides who are usually, but not always, deceased relatives. Often it is someone who was close to us while he or she was alive—a parent, sibling, or other close relative. It can be extremely comforting to know that people who have been important to you in the past are still there to guide and help you whenever you need it.

Many people are aware of the continual presence of their spirit guides. For instance, Sophia Peabody, the wife of Nathaniel Hawthorne, celebrated author of *The Scarlet Letter*, "was conscious of her mother's presence with her on momentous occasions."[1]

People have known about spirit guides for thousands of years. Throughout recorded history, shamans all around the world have been able to go into a trance state to ask for help from the spirits.

Perhaps the most famous historical account of a spirit guide is Socrates' Daimon, who continually provided him with advice and warned him of danger. Xenophon quoted Socrates in his *Apology*: "This prophetic voice has been heard by me throughout my life; it is certainly more trustworthy than omens from the flight or entrails of birds; I call it a God or a daimon. I have told my friends the warnings I have received, and up to now the voice has never been wrong."[2]

In the Holy Bible we read about King Saul paying a visit to a medium to receive a communication from the spirit of the prophet Samuel. The first book of Samuel, chapter 28, verse 7, says: "Then said Saul unto his servants, Seek me a woman that hath a familiar spirit, that I may go to her, and enquire of her. And his servants said to him, there is a woman that hath a familiar spirit at Endor." Saul disguised himself and went to see this woman, who produced the spirit of Samuel. Unfortunately for King Saul, the spirit predicted his impending death.

Saint Augustine wrote in his *De Cura Pro Mortuis*: "The spirits of the dead can be sent to the living and can unveil to them the future which they themselves have learned from other spirits or from angels, or by divine revelation."[3]

Spiritualist mediums often have guides who have been reincarnated many times and developed enormous wisdom. They are often Native American chiefs, Chinese sages, Egyptian priests and other wise people from past ages.

You are not restricted to just one spirit guide. You may start out with one guide and then move on to another as you progress and develop spiritually. Although you may not realize it, you have a number of guides helping you all the time, each with their own special talents and skills.

Spirit guides can be almost anyone, but usually they are highly evolved souls who have a desire to help people in this incarnation. Consequently, although there are many mischievous spirits, you will never find these acting as spirit guides.

Mischievous spirits often appear when people play with devices such as the ouija board without knowing much about them. The ouija board can be a useful instrument when used responsibly, but unfortunately it is promoted mainly as a parlor game, and it is not surprising that it attracts negative entities when used in this way.

Negative spirits have always been around, and the solution to any difficulties you have with them can be found in the Bible. The First Epistle of John, in chapter 4, verses 1–3, says:

> *Beloved, believe not every spirit, but try the spirits whether they are of God: because many false prophets are gone out into the world. Hereby know ye the Spirit of God: every spirit that confesseth that Jesus Christ is come in the flesh is of God: And every spirit that confesseth not that Jesus Christ is come in the flesh is not of God: and this is that spirit of antichrist, whereof ye have heard that it should come; and even now already is it in the world.*

When you meet a new spirit you should treat it with caution until you know exactly what sort of spirit it is. I am sure you do this when you meet new people, anyway. If you are in any doubt, ask the spirit whether it is of God, and see what response you get.

Spirit guides are usually contacted by a medium, or through a séance. It is possible to create a small séance just for yourself, but better results are usually obtained when a group of like-minded people work together.

The Growth of Spiritualism

Séances were at their most popular in the century leading up to World War II. Much of their success was due to the growth of spiritualism, which taught that survival after death could be proven, and that it was possible to communicate with people who had passed over.

Spiritualism began on March 31, 1848, in Hydesville, a tiny hamlet of less than forty homes in upstate New York. Two sisters, Kate and Margaret Fox, began communicating with strange rapping sounds that had been troubling the family for some months. Their father had spent a considerable amount of time trying to find the source of the noises, without success, though neighbors told him that the house was haunted. In fact, it was believed that ghosts had driven away the previous tenants.[4]

On the evening of March 31, the noises were occurring as usual. Kate, the youngest sister, was playing a game. She stopped, snapped her fingers together several times and called out, "Here, Mr. Splitfoot, do as I do!" The spirit immediately gave back the same number of taps. This horrified the girls' mother, who was in the room at the time. Mr. Splitfoot was a childish name for the Devil. However, Kate was not afraid. She went through the motions of snapping her fingers, and the correct number of raps came back. "Mother," Kate said, "It can *see* as well as hear!"

Mrs. Fox cautiously asked the spirit if it could count to ten. Immediately, it responded with ten raps. She then asked for the number of her living children. Four raps—the correct answer—were heard. Mrs. Fox got bolder. "Are you a man?" she asked. The spirit remained silent. "Are you a disembodied spirit that has taken possession of my dear children?" This time several loud raps were heard.

This was conclusive evidence as far as the Fox family was concerned. That same night, neighbors were invited in to hear the sounds and ask questions. The spirit was able to answer most of them correctly. On the following nights as many as three hundred people would crowd into the small house to hear the rapping sounds.

The sisters worked out a code to communicate more effectively with the spirit. Using this, the spirit was able to tell them that he was the ghost of Charles B. Rosma, a traveling salesman who had been murdered in the house and buried in the cellar.

Word of these exciting occurrences traveled quickly, and people flocked to see the Fox sisters and to witness the rapping sounds. E. E. Lewis' pamphlet, *A Report on the Mysterious Noises Heard in the House of John D. Fox, Hydesville, Arcadia, Wayne County*, appeared just a few months after the noises became public. He wrote: "Saturday and Sunday crowds come from far and near, filling the roads and lining the fences with horses and vehicles."

Family life changed drastically for the Fox family, and the parents decided to send the girls away to enable them to grow up away from all the fuss. Kate was sent to her brother's house in Auburn, and Margaret went to live with her older sister, Leah, in Rochester. Their popularity survived the moves and the girls created a huge interest in both Auburn and Rochester.

While living in Rochester, Margaret discovered that she could communicate with the spirits by automatic writing. This was a huge advance over the laborious process of decoding the number of raps that were produced.

On November 14, 1849, Leah Fox rented the Corinthian Hall for three nights and organized Margaret's first public meetings. The hall was packed each night with people who had paid twenty-five cents to attend. The audience was divided fairly equally. People either believed in the phenomena or were totally skeptical.

After the first evening, a committee was set up to investigate what had occurred, and to report back the following night. This committee announced that if there had been fraud, it had not been detected. This satisfied no one, and a second committee was formed. They reached the same conclusion. When a third committee also returned with the same verdict, the audience rioted and the police had to come in to ensure that Margaret and Leah were able to leave safely.

The publicity increased and the future of spiritualism was assured. The Fox sisters embarked on a tour of major cities, gaining converts everywhere they went. Other people discovered that they also possessed mediumistic talents, and séances became the craze of the day. Some of these people brought in innovations of their own, but most simply copied what the others did.

David P. Abbott reported: "As soon as the first mediums could induce the spirits of the departed to return to this earth and rap on tables and furniture, the fashion rapidly spread and mediums all over the country sprang up with exactly these same powers. The fashion remains to this day. … As soon as a leading medium started the fashion of having an Indian guide, all of the mediums in the country had Indian guides. Unto this day this fashion is still in vogue."[5]

In 1854, 15,000 spiritualists sent a petition to Congress asking for a commission to investigate the phenomenon. A year later George Templeton Strong wrote: "who could have predicted...that hundreds of thousands of people in this country would believe themselves able to communicate daily with the ghosts of their grandfathers?"[6] It is believed that within five years of the birth of spiritualism, 30,000 mediums were busy conducting séances.[7]

The purpose of these séances was to communicate with the dead. The medium and sitters would sit around a table in the dark, holding hands and singing hymns. After a while, a variety of strange things would occur. There would be various rapping noises, of course, but there might also be table-tipping, the arrival of "apports" (gifts from the spirit world), ectoplasm flowing from the medium's body, and even visible spirits.

Many people attended séances purely for their entertainment value. However, many of these people later became believers after experiencing a séance. Photography was in its infancy, and photographs of spirits floating in the air around the medium also encouraged belief in the phenomena.

Famous people became involved. Abraham Lincoln's wife, Mary, became interested in spiritualism after the death of her young son, Willie. She held many seances in the White House during the Civil War. She also spent many years attending séances in an attempt to contact her husband after his death. It is believed that Abraham Lincoln was equally interested in spiritualism. Certainly, he attended his wife's séances and is believed to have attended public séances while visiting New York. An article about his interest appeared in the *Cleveland Plain Dealer* before his death, and Lincoln never denied it.[8]

Spiritualism spread to England, and its growth proved just as rapid there as it had in the States. Even Queen Victoria attended a séance.

From the very beginning, many scientists were skeptical, but others attended séances and became convinced of their validity. One good example is that of Alfred Russel Wallace, who co-discovered the principle of natural selection with Charles Darwin. He reported that at a séance he attended all the sitters watched as the séance table became covered with fresh flowers and ferns. "The flowers appeared on the polished table dimly visible as a something, before we lighted the gas. When we did so the whole surface of the four-feet circular table was covered with fresh flowers and ferns, a sight so beautiful and marvellous, that in the course of a not uneventful life I can hardly recall anything that has more strongly impressed me. I begged that nothing be touched till we had carefully examined them. The first thing that struck us all was their extreme freshness and beauty. The next that they were all covered, especially the ferns, with a delicate dew."[9] The scientific interest culminated in the formation of the Society for Psychical Research in 1882.

Some mediums always worked through a single spirit guide. Others, however, used many. One of the most famous of these was Hélène Smith,[10] a French spiritualist medium who practiced around the turn of the century. She had numerous guides who would possess her body when she went into a trance. One of these was the spirit of a dead Martian. With her Martian in control she would speak and write in Martian, and even drew Martian landscapes.[11] In other words, she was "channeling" her Martian some eighty years before channeling became popular.

Incidentally, Hélène Smith's mother was also psychic and could see angels. In 1870, Hélène's younger sister was ill and her mother got up during the night to attend to her. She saw a shining angel with arms outstretched standing by the small child's bed. Mme. Smith woke her husband, but the angel had vanished by the time he got up. Although the doctor had assured the family that the girl would recover, she died the following day.[12]

Spiritualism was also helped enormously by the work of Andrew Jackson Davis (1826–1910), known as the Poughkeepsie Seer. John Nevil Maskelyne called him the pioneer of modern spiritualism because his writings became the support and basis of much of the movement.

Davis had clairvoyant abilities from childhood, but they really blossomed after he heard a lecture on mesmerism when he was seventeen. He began experimenting with a friend and found that when he was in a trance state he could diagnose illnesses, in the same way that Edgar Cayce could a century later.

When he was eighteen, Davis was visited by the spirits of Galen, the ancient Greek physician, and Emanuel Swedenborg, the Swedish mystic and philosopher. Both told Davis that he was in this incarnation to perform an important mission.

Shortly after this experience, the Reverend William Fishbough took Davis to New York and transcribed everything Davis said while in a trance state. The first fifteen months of these sessions appeared as *The Principles of Nature, Her Divine Revelations, and a Voice to Mankind.* This huge book of some eight hundred pages became a bestseller in 1847 and thirty-four editions of it appeared in the following thirty years. Davis was just twenty-one at the time.

In this book Davis claimed that Jesus was a great prophet and teacher, but could not claim to be divine. He saw the universe as a harmonious whole, in which each individual soul is constantly progressing and growing. This lifetime on earth, he said, was simply a pause on the way to "Summer-Land."

Davis described Summer-Land in detail. It consists of a magnificent garden with trees, flowers, birds, and temples situated in breathtaking landscapes. The inhabitants enjoy music, great banquets, and many societies, catering to every possible interest. It is a place of great joy and happiness.

Three types of spirits live there. The spirits of people who have died recently go to Summer-Land. Next, there are "angels," highly advanced spirits whose task is to help the people living on earth. Finally there are mischievous spirits, who are not bad or evil; they are simply at a lower level of development than the other spirits. Every spirit finally finds its "spiritual mate," or soul-mate, in Summer-Land.

Davis declared that it was a sign of great wisdom to ask the spirits for advice. People who doubted the existence of spirits were not yet ready to progress spiritually.

In his book Davis wrote: "It is a truth that spirits commune with one another while one is in the body and the other is in the higher spheres—and this, too, when the person in the body is unconscious of the influx, and hence cannot be convinced of the fact; and this truth will ere long present itself in the form of a living demonstration. And the world will hail with delight the ushering-in of that era when the interiors of men will be opened, and the spiritual communion will be established such as is now being enjoyed by the inhabitants of Mars, Jupiter, and Saturn."[13]

Unfortunately, this ideal world never came to be, and spiritualism began a slow decline, mainly because many mediums were detected in fraud. Harry Houdini, the famous magician, played a large part in this. He was distraught when his mother died and tried everything he could to contact her. However, everywhere he went he found fraudulent mediums. This so infuriated him that he spent much of the rest of his life exposing them.

Home and Later Mediums

Unquestionably, the most famous medium of all was Daniel Dunglas Home (1833–86). Hereward Carrington wrote: "though Home was under far more careful and prolonged scrutiny than any other medium, fraud was never detected at any of Home's séances, nor was it ever suspected on any occasion."[14]

Home was born in Edinburgh, Scotland, and was adopted by a childless aunt who took him to the United States. He discovered his psychic powers as a child and at the age of thirteen experienced his first vision when he foresaw the death of a school friend. Home later communicated with this boy's spirit. In 1850, he knew clairvoyantly that his mother in Scotland would die three days before it happened. His aunt became disturbed at the rapping sounds coming from his room and, believing that he was possessed by the devil, asked three ministers to exorcise him. This changed nothing and his aunt asked him to leave home.

For the next five years Home traveled widely, living with people who wanted to help him develop his gifts. By all accounts, he was an exceptionally charming man and became a popular house guest of the wealthy. People enjoyed his private séances where all the usual manifestations would occur. Rapping sounds would be heard, tables would tilt, bells would ring and spirit hands would appear.

However, even at this young age Home had the first of a number of exclusive items available to make his séances different from everyone else's. He had an accordion that was played by the spirits. Home would hold the accordion under the table by the non-playing end, and in the dark the spirits would play music on it. Ultimately, this accordion was able to float in the air while playing "Home Sweet Home" or "The Last Rose of Summer."

Home learned from this the value of having something different to offer. In later years he would demonstrate how he could handle red-hot coals using spirit protection. He could elongate himself and conduct feats of levitation. Sometimes the sitters were levitated while still sitting in their chairs, and at other times Home himself would levitate.

It was the Ashley Place Levitation that ensured Home's lasting place in the history of spiritualism. On either December 13 or 16, 1868, Home was conducting a séance for three sitters in the London apartment of Viscount Adare. While in a trance, he went to the next room and opened a window. He then levitated himself out the window and returned to his sitters through the window in their room. Viscount Adare wrote: "We heard Home go into the next room, heard the window being thrown up, and presently Home appeared standing upright outside our window. He opened the window and walked in quite coolly."

The sitters were, not surprisingly, amazed at this feat and Viscount Adare said that he could not understand how Home had done it. Home then told Adare to move back a bit. "He then went through the open space head first quite rapidly, his body being nearly horizontal and quite rigid. He came in again feet foremost."[15] The space between the two windows was seven feet, four inches, the window ledges were only four inches wide, and the windows were some seventy feet above the ground, making trickery an unlikely explanation.

Two of the three witnesses were leading members of London society: Lord Lindsay (later Earl of Crawford) and Viscount Adare (later Earl of Dunraven). The other witness was Captain Charles Wynne, Adare's cousin. Sir Arthur Conan Doyle declared that the testimony of the three witnesses was "unimpeachable." The three witnesses wrote up an account of the incident, which became the talk of London.

Home was also tested by Sir William Crookes, a leading scientist of the day. Crookes and a group of his friends asked Home to conduct a séance for them in 1871. At this séance Home partially levitated himself, thrust his hands into the fire, and removed a glowing coal, and his famous accordion played tunes.[16] Sir William later tested Home further by placing the accordion inside a cage under the table. This made no difference, and the accordion played as sweetly as ever. In an article for the January 1874 *Quarterly Journal of Science*, Crookes wrote:

> *There are at least a hundred recorded instances of* Mr. *Home's rising from the ground, in the presence of as many separate persons, and I have heard from the lips of the three witnesses to the most striking occurrence of this kind—the Earl of Dunraven, Lord Lindsay, and Captain* C. *Wynne—their own most minute accounts of what took place. To reject the recorded evidence on this*

> *subject is to reject all human testimony whatever; for no fact in sacred or profane history is supported by a stronger array of proofs.*[17]

Home married a wealthy Russian noblewoman in 1871 and moved to France, where he virtually retired. In 1873 he published a book called *Lights and Shadows of Spiritualism*, which exposed the methods of fraudulent mediums. He died of tuberculosis on June 21, 1886. His tombstone in St. Germain, Paris, is inscribed: "To another discerning of Spirits."

The influence of spiritualism has gradually faded over the last century. However, spirit guides have been around for thousands of years and will continue to play an influential role in our future. Today, channeling is by far the most popular way of contacting spirit guides and, like Hélène Smith, the popular French medium at the turn of the century, many channelers contact spirits from other planets, as well as lost continents.

Channeling has one important major difference to mediumship. Mediums, with few exceptions, make contact with human spirits. Channelers contact a huge variety of spirits: humans, angels, dolphins and other animals, Ascended Masters, and people from other planets.

By far the most famous channeler of this century was Edgar Cayce (1877–1945), a gentle, humble humanitarian who could enter into a trance state and give incredibly detailed medical diagnoses for people as far as hundreds of miles away.

His worldwide fame began in 1910, when the *New York Times* ran a two-page story about his successes as a clairvoyant healer. From that time on he was kept busy, with people all over the world wanting healing and advice from the "sleeping prophet." When he died he left a legacy of more than fourteen million words, the result of readings for more than ten thousand people. His work is being kept alive by the Association for Research and Enlightenment at Virginia Beach.

Channelers are able to switch off their conscious and subconscious minds temporarily. This enables them to channel information directly from the superconscious. This information comes through a discarnate entity who appears to take over the consciousness of the channeler temporarily. No one knows exactly who or what these entities are. They have been called angels, spirits, spirit guides, and even God.

In the next chapter we will start communicating with our spirit guides using a variety of time-tested methods.

12

Ways to Contact Spirit Guides

Many people expect to see or hear their spirit guides using their eyes and ears. In fact, this is rarely the case. Our guides communicate to us telepathically and spiritually. Consequently, we need to develop our spiritual vision in order to see them clearly. Often the message comes through as a faint, almost imperceptible intuition. Many times a message from your guide will seem exactly like a thought and only later will you realize it came from your guide. If you are not open to receiving messages from your guides, they will remain unheard.

You need to be able to stand outside your own thinking and feeling patterns to make contact with your spirit guides. This is difficult for most people, though many of the best mediums are able to dissociate themselves in a matter of seconds, any time they choose. In fact, one medium jokingly said: "I am a loose woman," because she could instantly free herself to be open to the spirit world whenever she chose.[1]

Because it is not easy to achieve this state of positive awareness, mediums have used a variety of devices to help them. The most popular—and practical—of these have always been the ouija board, automatic writing, table-tipping, and the pendulum. They were all favorite methods of communicating with the spirit world in the golden age of spiritualism. Many spiritualists, including Hélène Smith, produced spirit writing in their séances while under the influence of their spirit guides.

Planchettes and Ouija Boards

The planchette is believed to have been invented by a French spiritualist, M. Planchette, in 1853.[2] The traditional planchette consists of a small triangular or heart-shaped plate with a small wheel or ball bearing on two of the three corners. The third corner of the triangle is supported by a pencil. This device is placed on a large piece of paper and one or more people place their fingers on it. The planchette will start to move, creating a pencil trail that might create a scribble, a picture, or—more usually—words. The planchette works best with one or two people working it at a time. If too many people place their fingers on it, the result is likely to be just a scribble.

After a while, people discovered that they could save time by writing the letters of the alphabet around the edge of the paper and have the planchette spell out words, one letter at a time.

This is the principle of the ouija board. The name *ouija* comes from *oui* and *ja*, the French and German words for *yes*. In practice the board contains both the words *yes* and *no*, as well as the letters of the alphabet, and frequently numbers from zero to nine. The original planchette used with the ouija board contained three wheels, as the pencil was not required. Now, most planchettes are made of plastic rather than wood, and have a small felt pad, instead of wheels, at the end of each leg.

The ouija board as we know it today was invented around 1892 by Elijah J. Bond and William Fuld in Baltimore. Parker Brothers, Inc., purchased all the rights in 1966, and have since sold millions of Ouija Boards.[3]

Many people think that the ouija board is a modern invention, but something similar was being used by Pythagoras in 540 B.C.E. He conducted séances in which a special table on wheels would move toward different signs, much like a planchette on a ouija board. Pythagoras and his pupil, Philolaus, would then interpret these messages from the spirit world for their audiences.[4]

My mother frequently used an improvised ouija board. She would arrange pieces of paper containing the letters of the alphabet in a circle on the kitchen table, and place an upturned glass in the center. She would then rest two fingers on the glass, take a deep breath, and ask the first question. As soon as she did, the glass would start racing over the smooth surface of the table, and she would sometimes have to repeat the question, because the glass moved too quickly for her to pick up all of the letters indicated.

Using a Planchette

To use a planchette or ouija board you need to be loose and relaxed. A feeling of expectation or anticipation helps, too. It is best to have one or two people operating the planchette, with another person to write down the letters as they come, as the planchette can move extremely quickly once it gets going. However, you can do it entirely on your own, as well.

Make sure that everyone is relaxed, but in a state of anticipation. Ask, "Is anyone there?" and see what the board answers. If the planchette indicates "no," it is better to stop right away and try again later. Naturally, if it answers "yes," you can continue. A good second question is, "Have you a message for anyone?" Find out who the message is for, and then carry on to receive the message. With practice, you will find that the ouija board can answer questions almost as quickly as you can write them down.

In her book *Moments of Knowing*, Ann Bridge recounted an interesting story concerning the ouija board. Some friends of hers had rented a farmhouse on the moors of Cornwall. They, in turn, re-rented it and asked a friend to keep an eye on it for them. This man, Will Arnold-Foster, went up to check on the house one evening and found the occupants sitting around the table, experimenting with an improvised ouija board and upturned glass. They invited him to join them in the circle. He refused, but agreed to stay and write down the messages that might be received.

As soon as they had begun, the glass announced that it had a message for Ruth. None of the occupants knew a Ruth, but Will knew a Ruth Mallory, the widow of George Mallory, who had died on the slopes of Mount Everest.

Becoming a little bit more interested, Will asked them to ask who the message was from. The glass replied, "George." Will quickly said, "George who?" and the glass responded, "George Mallory."

Suddenly, everyone was interested, as the tragedy on Everest was still fairly recent. However, Will was the only person in the room who knew that George Mallory's widow was called Ruth.

Will asked what the message for Ruth was. The glass said, "Tell her she must do something about Frank."

This puzzled Will, as he knew the names of Mallory's brother and three children. None were named "Frank." He asked more questions, but the only reply was: "He's unhappy—she must do something about him."

Will wrote a letter to Ruth, telling her the message. He apologized for bothering her, as he was sure the message must be nonsense.

In fact, the message was genuine and useful. During World War I, the Mallorys had looked after a young boy from Vienna named Franz. He had stayed with them for three or four years, and then been sent back to his mother. On receiving the ouija board message, Ruth realized that "Frank" must mean "Franz." She made inquiries in Vienna and found that the boy was in great need. She arranged for him to come back to England and brought him up as her own.[5]

Whole books have been produced one letter at a time on the ouija board. The most famous instance of this is Patience Worth. In 1913, two young women in St. Louis were conducting experiments with a ouija board. A friend had introduced them to the board and they had spent many hours fascinated with the progress of the planchette as it spelled out unimportant messages. However, on the evening of July 8, the women received a shock when the board spelled out: "Many moons ago I lived. Again I come. Patience Worth my name."

The two women, twenty-one-year-old Pearl Curran and her friend Emily Hutchings, gasped and stared at each other. The planchette started moving again and spelled out: "Wait. I would speak with thee. If thou shalt live, then so shall I. I make my bread by thy hearth. Good friends, let us be merrie. The time for work is past. Let the tabbie drowse and blink her wisdom to the fire-log."

Gradually, the two women discovered that Patience Worth was an English Quaker who had lived in the seventeenth century. Her personality was so charming, amusing and forceful that the two women immediately began recording everything that Patience Worth spelled out.

They soon discovered that it was essential for Pearl Curran to have her hand on the planchette. Two people were required every time, but it made no difference who the second person was. Mrs. Curran has been described as "a young woman of nervous temperament, bright, vivacious, ready of speech. She has a taste for literature, but is not a writer, and has never attempted to write anything more ambitious than a personal letter."[6] All the same, over a period of time, Patience Worth, through Pearl Curran's ouija board, produced six novels, several plays, and more than four thousand poems. An anthology of the "best" poetry of 1917 included five poems by Patience Worth, and only three each by two leading poets of the day, Amy Lowell and Vachel Lindsay.

Patience Worth's work received excellent reviews. The *New York Times* described one of her books as "remarkable." In another review, the same paper said: "Notwithstanding the serious quality and the many pitifulnesses and tragedies of the story it tells, the book has much humor of a quaint, demure kind, a kind of humor that stands out as characteristic of all her work and her personality…the plot is contrived with such skill, deftness and ingenuity as many a novelist in the flesh might envy."[7]

Pearl Curran never went into a trance while using her ouija board. She was always relaxed and at ease, and even engaged in conversation with other people in the room while the planchette moved around the board. The movements were in no way affected by what was going on in the room at the time.

Naturally, there were many people who doubted that Patience Worth ever existed or was a spirit. She did not care. She made fun of the people who came to watch and even composed a small poem to give to people who insisted that she prove herself to be real:

A phantom? Well enough
Prove thee thyself to be.
I say, behold, here I be—
Buskins, kirtle, cap, and pettyskirts,
And much tongue.
Weel, what hast thou to prove thee?[8]

After some years of using the ouija board, Pearl Curran discovered that she could simply speak the letters aloud as they popped into her mind, while a friend recorded the results.

Very few people have been able to produce anywhere near the quantity or quality of work that Pearl Curran produced through her ouija board. I have been privileged to read some remarkable writings that have come through this way, but I have also had the misfortune of wading through a large amount of virtual rubbish.

It took Patience Worth six months before she started transmitting more than fragments. Be patient and do not expect words of genius to come from your ouija board until you have had a great deal of practice.

Automatic Writing

Automatic writing is a means of communication using pen and paper. The pen moves over the page directed by a power other than the conscious mind of the person holding it. Originally, automatic writing was done using a planchette with two wheels and a pencil. However, writing produced this way is extremely hard to decipher, and before long someone discovered that it was much easier simply to hold a pen or pencil in the hand.

In his book *Spirit Identity*, William Stainton Moses (1839–1892) described his first experience with automatic writing:

> *My right arm was seized about the middle of the forearm, and dashed violently up and down with a noise resembling that of a number of paviors at work. It was the most tremendous exhibition of 'unconscious muscular action' I ever saw. In vain I tried to stop it. I distinctly felt the grasps, soft and firm, round my arm, and though perfectly possessed of senses and volition, I was powerless to interfere, although my hand was disabled for some days by the bruising it then got.*[9]

William Howitt (1792–1879), a well-known English spiritualist, experimented with automatic writing after seeing his son and daughter successfully doing it. In January 1858, after visiting a Mrs. Wilkinson, who was able to draw automatic pictures in the same way, he picked up a pencil and paper. His daughter described the experience in her book *Pioneers of Spiritual Reformation*:

> *My father had not sat many minutes passive, holding a pencil in his hand upon a sheet of paper, ere something resembling an electric shock ran through his arm and hand; whereupon the pencil began to move in circles. The influence becoming stronger and stronger, moved not alone the hand, but the whole arm in a rotatory motion, until the arm was at length raised, and rapidly—as if it had been the spoke of a wheel propelled by machinery—whirled irresistibly in a wide sweep, and with great speed, for some ten minutes through the air. The effect of this rapid rotation was felt by him in the muscles of the arm for some time afterwards. Then the arm being again at rest the pencil, in the passive fingers, began gently, but clearly and decidedly, to move.*[10]

Most people find that it takes time to become adept at automatic writing. However, persistence pays off, and once the ability has been developed the words can come extremely quickly. The Reverend George Vale Owen (1869–1931) received words at an average rate of twenty-four a minute, four nights a week, for months on end.[11]

An interesting example of automatic writing occurred in England in 1908. Frederick Bligh Bond was in charge of the excavations of the old ruined abbey at Glastonbury. He enlisted the aid of Captain John Bartlett, a well-known medium and channel. John Bartlett used automatic writing to initiate contact with the spirit of a medieval monk who was able to tell Bond exactly where to find the missing Edgar Chapel and the remains of a destroyed shrine that were buried beneath the abbey ruins. The writing that came through was in Latin and Middle English.[12]

Later, John Bartlett used his talents at automatic drawing to create eight pictures of Glastonbury Abbey when it was complete. It is impossible to determine nowadays if his drawings are correct, but they conform to what is now known about the buried remains. It is interesting to note that John Bartlett used his left hand for these drawings, even though he was right-handed.[13]

Mediums were kept busy throughout World War I as distressed people tried to contact their dead relatives. A number of books produced through the ouija board, automatic writing, and table-tipping were published, and some became bestsellers.

Raymond, or Life and Death by Sir Oliver Lodge is the most notable example.[14] In 1915, when Lodge's son Raymond was fighting in Flanders, the famous medium Lenore Piper received a message that contained a quotation from the classical Roman poet, Horace. Lodge took this quote to mean that something bad was about to happen. On September 15, Lodge and his wife heard that their son had been killed in action. A week later, a friend of theirs who had also lost a son, and had since established an automatic writing connection with him, received a message for the Lodges: "I have seen that boy, Sir Oliver Lodge's son; he's better and has had a splendid rest, tell his people." Lady Lodge contacted Gladys Osborne Leonard, another well-known medium of the day, and made an appointment. At this session, a table tipped out a message: "Tell father I have met some friends of his…Yes, Myers."[15] In another session, Gladys Leonard went into a trance and brought back further messages from Raymond, describing life on the other side. Sir Oliver compiled all of the information that came through and published it in his book.

In 1918, a book called *Private Dowding*, composed entirely by automatic writing, was published. This book also became a bestseller and provided comfort for many who had lost relatives in World War I. The book told the story of a young English schoolteacher, Thomas Dowding, who was killed by shrapnel in France. Dowding's words were transcribed by the English medium W. T. Poole.[16]

Experimenting with Automatic Writing

As with the ouija board, it is essential to be relaxed when you wish to experiment with automatic writing. Sit somewhere comfortable with your writing arm creating a ninety-degree angle at the elbow. The hand holding the pen or pencil should be comfortably resting on the paper. (It is worth mentioning that some people have better results using the hand that they do not normally write with. I use my normal hand and have no success with my other hand, but some people do. You might want to try using the other hand to see what happens.)

Remain relaxed and simply wait to see what happens. Many people prefer to have their eyes closed at this stage, and go into a meditative state.

After a while, the hand holding the writing implement will start to move. Resist the temptation to look at what is happening, or even to show any interest. Automatic writing is unconscious writing, and any conscious interest will destroy the spontaneity and flow of the writing.

You may be fortunate and find that you start writing words and sentences from the outset. Most people start by drawing circles and ellipses. You may even write some words or phrases in mirror writing. It makes no difference what your hand draws or writes. As long as it creates something, you have made a good start. However, you will find that on occasion, nothing is produced, even after you have been doing it successfully for several months. Do not worry about this. It simply means that nothing is available to come through at that time. Simply put the implements away and try again on another occasion.

Practice regularly and you will be amazed at what you produce. You will quickly discover that it is truly "automatic" and your hand is impelled by an outside force that works better when your conscious mind is out of the way. You will also discover that you can write in this way for hours on end without becoming physically tired.

The writing you produce can be almost anything. You might create poems, novels, answers to questions that are troubling you, or spiritual insights. Do not evaluate anything while it is being produced. Simply record it. You can make time to evaluate and question afterwards.

Some people are able to create automatic writing while doing other things, such as reading or watching television. All you need do is have your pen and paper in position while you concentrate on some other activity.

Alfred, Lord Tennyson, William Butler Yeats, and Gertrude Stein are just a few of the many authors who have used automatic writing to expand their creativity. In fact, some people with no apparent creative talents have produced remarkable work through automatic writing. The philosopher C. H. Broad wrote in his preface to a book created by automatic writing: "There is, undoubtedly, some independent evidence for the existence, in some few persons, of remarkable creative and dramatizing powers, which reveal themselves only when their possessor is in a dissociated state." [17]

Ruth Montgomery wrote a series of books based on information passed on to her by her spirit guides. After meditating for a while, she would sit at her typewriter with her eyes closed, and for fifteen minutes her guides would use her fingers to type out the information they wanted to convey.[18]

Drawings, paintings, and even music have been created using automatic writing. Rosemary Brown, a London widow who is in touch with the spirits of Bach, Beethoven, Brahms, Chopin, Debussy, Liszt, Schubert, Stravinsky, and others, has produced many compositions in their styles using automatic writing. Sometimes she is guided by these composers on her piano, while at other times it is written down using automatic writing.

A few people have been able use automatic writing as a general aid in daily life. The best known of these was W. T. Stead (1849–1912), a leading journalist and human rights campaigner. He found that he could sit down and let his hand write his letters for him. He claimed that his automatic writing never let him down.

At one time, Stead was getting ready to meet a friend who did some journalism work for him. The friend had told him that her train would arrive at "about three." Before leaving for the station he mentally asked his friend to take control of his hand and give him a more accurate time for the train's arrival. The automatic writing produced said the train would arrive at ten minutes to three.

Stead went to the station and found that the train had been delayed. He took pencil and paper out of his pocket and again asked his friend: "Why the mischief have you been so late?"

His hand wrote: "We were detained at Middlesborough for so long; I do not know why."

When the train arrived a few minutes later, he asked his friend why it was late. "I do not know," she replied. "The train stopped so long at Middlesborough, it seemed as if it would never start."[19]

You will find automatic writing becoming more and more useful to you as time goes by. You will receive answers to questions and problems that have been bothering you.

You will receive insights that will enhance your spiritual awareness, and you will be able to help others by using your automatic writing skills to answer their questions.

Table-Tipping

Table-tipping became a phenomenon in France in the mid-nineteenth century. It was great fun to have a dinner party and afterwards have the guests see if they could make the table tap out messages. One tap of a table leg meant "yes," two taps meant "no," and three taps meant "maybe." Complete messages could be sent through a laborious process of spelling out words, one letter at a time.

A leading French doctor, Dr. Hippolyte Rivail (1804–1869), became annoyed with the popularity of table-tipping, particularly after the spirits began giving medical advice. He organized a group of people to visit the different salons where table-tipping was taking place and ask a specific set of questions. Afterwards, the group met to compare answers. Rivail was mystified to find that the answers, although expressed in different ways, were all the same. He had expected them all to be different.

This convinced Dr. Rivail. He continued experimenting and was told by the spirits to call himself Allan Kardec. Apparently, he had been both Allan and Kardec in previous incarnations. Under the name of Allan Kardec he published many books including *The Spirits' Book* (1856), *The Medium's Book* (1861), and *The Gospel as*

Explained by Spirits (1864). His books created a sensation in Europe, and some of them are still in print today. He coined the word *spiritism*, which became the European version of *spiritualism*.

Practicing Table-Tipping

You can use any table at all for table-tipping. However, it is best to start with a lightweight table, preferably a circular one with just three legs. This will get you off to a good start. Once you have successfully tilted a small table, you can then progress to heavier and larger tables if you wish.

Choose someone to communicate with the table. It is very hard to get satisfactory results when everyone is asking questions at the same time.

Remove all the rugs from the floor. Although you can tilt tables over any surface, it is easier to do it on a linoleum or bare wood floor. You may also want to place all the other furniture around the walls, as once the table starts to move it can be difficult to control.

You will need at least three people to perform the experiment. Have them all sit around the table and place their fingertips lightly on the table top, with the tips of their thumbs touching. Their little fingers should also touch those of the people on either side. This creates a ring of energy that completely encircles the table.

Have someone dim the lights. In the pause that follows, you, or whoever has been chosen to communicate with the table, might want to say a prayer out loud, recite a poem, or have everyone sing an appropriate song. After this, the spokesperson can ask: "Is anyone there?"

Hopefully, this is all that will be required to start the table tipping. If nothing happens, wait a minute or two and ask the question again. I have never had to wait longer than ten minutes for the table to start moving. Usually, it happens in about a minute. The important thing is to remain patient. Although the experiment is serious, it should be done in a spirit of fun.

Once the table starts to move, the spokesperson can ask a variety of questions. It is best to start by asking if the spirit is a good spirit. Naturally, there is no way of knowing the quality of the spirit that will come through. If you get a low-grade or mischievous spirit, it is better to stop right away, rather than run the risk of damaging furniture with a violent table, or offending your guests with the information that might come through.

Ask the spirit if it has a message for someone in the room. If it answers positively, you can find out who the message is for, by asking further questions.

You can ask who the spirit is. Usually, it will be a relative of someone in the room, but it could just as easily be someone who is not known to anyone present.

Detailed answers can be found in one of two ways. You can ask the table to spell out the words by giving the correct number of taps to indicate the letter. One tap, for instance, would mean "A," two taps "B," three taps "C," and so on. However, with the noise created by the movement of the table it is not always easy to determine the correct letter. After receiving a letter, the spokesperson needs to confirm it by repeating the final letter. The whole process is made much simpler if the spokesperson simply calls out each letter of the alphabet as the table indicates it. If, for example, the letter is "F," the spokesperson would say: "A, B, C, D, E, F…F."

The other way is simply to guess at the letters. "Is it a P?" Two taps. "Is it a Q?" Two taps. "Is it an R?" One tap, meaning yes. Sometimes you will find that you end up with a strange word that makes no sense. This could mean that the spirit is tired or is simply having fun with you. Ask if it wants to continue. If it has had enough, there is no point in continuing, as you will receive nonsensical answers.

Occasionally, there are instances when a table moves, even when it is not supposed to. The famous Florence Cook, called "one of the most accomplished mediums who ever lived" by Sir Arthur Conan Doyle, caused tables to move everywhere she went. Gambier Bolton, in *Psychic Force*, wrote: "During any meal with Mrs. Elgie Corner (Florence Cook)…the heavy dining table will commence first to quiver, setting all the glasses shaking, and plates, knives, forks and spoons in motion, and then to rock and sway from side to side, occasionally going so far as to tilt up at one end or at one side; and all the time raps and tappings will be heard in the table and in many different parts of the room. Taking a meal with her in a public restaurant is a somewhat serious matter."[20]

Table-tipping is great fun, and is an excellent way of introducing people to the concept of spirits. I have found that as long as one person around the table believes, it makes no difference if the others are skeptical, or even opposed. However, if everyone at the table is skeptical, the table will not move.

The Pendulum

Pendulums[21] have been used for thousands of years—at least since Roman times, when they were used to forecast the outcomes of battles.[22]

A pendulum is a small solid object suspended from a cord or chain. Many people use their wedding rings, suspended from a length of cotton. A number of people have told me that for psychic work the cord needs to be made of silk. Because of the number of times I have been asked about this, I conducted a series of experiments and found that the material used makes no difference at all.

The cord is held between the thumb and first finger of the hand. If you are right-handed, use your right hand. Naturally, use your left hand if you are left-handed. If you are going to ask a series of questions, it is better to rest the elbow of this hand on the table.

Start by holding the weight to stop the pendulum from swinging. Ask it which movement indicates "yes." Let go of the weight and see what the pendulum does. It will move in one of four ways. It may go from side to side, or towards and away from you. It may also move in a circular direction, either clockwise or counterclockwise.

Once you have the movement for "yes," you can ask which direction indicates "no." This still leaves two directions. You can use one for "I don't know" and the other for "I don't want to answer."

For psychic work, start by asking if anyone is there. If the answer is positive, you can start asking questions in the same way as the other methods. I prefer to ask the questions out loud, as this forces me to frame my request in the form of a question. If you think the question, rather than speak it, make sure that your mind is clearly focused on a specific question and can hold that thought until the pendulum has provided an answer.

When you are finished, thank the pendulum for its help and put it away carefully. You will get better results if you treat it with respect.

A few years ago I witnessed an interesting example. Some skeptical friends asked me to demonstrate my pendulum for them. It worked well as long as they asked sensible questions, but it absolutely refused to move as soon as they started asking frivolous questions. I thanked it for its help and put it away.

The major disadvantage of the pendulum is that, if you are emotionally involved in the outcome, it will give you the answers that you want. In these cases, you will get more accurate results by asking someone who has no emotional involvement in the outcome to hold the pendulum and ask the questions. I find it best to leave the room, and sometimes even the house, to avoid subconsciously influencing the movement of the pendulum while the other person is asking the questions.

Other Methods of Communication

You can receive answers from your spirit guides in many different ways. An acquaintance of mine always looks forward to autumn because she receives messages from her guides from the fallen leaves. This is an example of psychometry. Her neighbors think she is crazy as she picks up the fallen leaves one at a time, but she somehow receives messages from her guides through the leaves. She also keeps the autumn leaves until next fall to ensure contact all year round. Members of her family regularly find leaves in different drawers and cupboards in their home.

Telepathy is another common way of receiving messages. One moment you may have no idea how a certain problem will be solved, and a few seconds later the answer simply appears in your mind. As the answer was not there earlier, the solution must be the result of a telepathic communication from your spirit guide to you.

I have frequently received messages from friends and strangers that have been arranged by my guides. I am sure you have had the experience of telling a complete stranger more than you would tell someone you know well. Somehow, it often seems easier to unburden oneself to a stranger. Sometimes, the stranger will respond with some good, sound advice that provides insight or answers a question that has been bothering us. In these instances, our guides have been working through other people to help us.

I was 12,000 miles from home when I heard that my father had died. I spent the next several hours wandering around in a virtual daze. Late in the day, a woman came up to me in the street and spoke to me kindly and gently. No doubt she was able to see that something had occurred from my body language and expression, but I believe that it was a spirit guide who had encouraged her to cross the road and speak to me.

Some years ago I was researching a book and tried to find an expert on a particular subject. I turned on the television set and the program was an interview with someone discussing the very subject I was trying to learn about. I never watch afternoon television, but on this day something impelled me to turn the set on. Obviously, this must have been the result of a spirit guide leading me in the right direction.

Not long ago I was trying to find the source of a particular quotation. I consulted a book of quotations and accidentally knocked another book off the shelves. Amazingly enough, it landed open on the very page that contained the quote I was looking for. Again, this must have been my spirit guides helping me. Once you start looking for instances like this you will find that many apparent coincidences are the result of your spirit guides quietly and efficiently helping you.

Communication can come in surprising ways, but we must be prepared to listen. Jane, a friend of mine, was devastated when her current boyfriend vanished without saying goodbye. She was convinced that he would return with a good explanation, and that everything would be all right. As she was discussing this with a group of friends, the four-year-old son of one of them raised his head from the game he was playing and said, "He's not coming back." He said the words with absolute conviction and immediately returned to his game. "If it hadn't been for the way he spoke, I would have ignored him," Jane told me. "After all, he was just a little kid!"

Yet the boy was right. Jane's boyfriend had been involved in a complicated confidence scheme and had suddenly left town. She never saw or heard from him again. Obviously, Jane's spirit guide was talking to her through the small child.

Communication can work both ways, of course. We can ask our spirit guides to help us, and other people, through intermediaries. If you feel that a certain friend, for instance, needs some encouragement or help, you can ask your spirit guide to cause someone else to tell your friend the words that need to be said.

I have done this with friends who were having a difficult time in their marriage. Although they loved each other dearly, they had almost stopped communicating and seemed to be drifting apart. I knew that Madeleine desperately wanted Jeff to tell her how much he loved her. Jeff adored her, but found it impossible to say the simple words "I love you." I asked my guide to help Jeff say the three magic words that had the power to save their relationship. Deep down I was convinced that it was too late to save the situation, but one night Jeff came home with a bunch of flowers and a bottle of wine and told Madeleine how much he loved her. More than twenty years later they are still together, and I am certain they will remain deeply in love with each other forever.

We also communicate with our spirit guides in our sleep. Most of the time we do this without realizing it, but it is possible to use this valuable time to receive the answers we need.

When you are lying in bed waiting for sleep, think about the different questions you want your guides to answer. It makes no difference how many questions you may have, but you must formulate each one into a specific question. You may be worried about something that is happening at work. It may not be anything you can pinpoint exactly, but you have a feeling that something is not right. Knowing this much is useful, but to obtain a specific, detailed answer from your guide you need to phrase it in the form of a question. You might ask, "Will the situation at work improve next week?" or "Will the tension at work ease over the next few days?"

Once you have asked the question, relax and allow yourself to fall asleep confident that your question will be answered. Usually, the answer will pop into your mind as soon as you wake up. However, it may occur later on in the day. Do not be concerned if it takes longer than that. It simply means that the question is taking time to answer. Ask the question again before going to sleep the following night, and continue to do this every night until you receive an answer. It is important that you remain calm and confident that you will receive a reply.

One elderly lady I know, who has been a medium for some sixty years, told me that she communicates with her guides through her soul. "I can feel the information welling up inside me before it comes into my conscious mind," she explained. "My guides don't communicate the way we do, using words. They express themselves telepathically. Sometimes a message will simply appear in my mind, but more often, it enters my soul before reaching my mind."

Finally, another extremely effective way of making contact with your spirit guides is through silence. This is similar to meditation, but in this instance you are trying to still your mind completely to allow any messages from your guides simply to flow into your consciousness. In meditation we are usually focused on a specific mantra or phrase. With this technique we are trying to focus on nothing at all. This method is difficult at first, because we are not used to quieting our minds completely. An excellent way of practicing this technique is immediately after a progressive relaxation, when you are completely relaxed physically. Tell your mind to be still and then wait to see what happens.

The first few times you try this, you are likely to start thinking about all sorts of things within a few seconds. However, with practice, you will be able to lengthen the period of stillness gradually until you can last three or four minutes without a conscious thought. Your guides will be able to communicate with you very easily once you can reach this state.

You may find that you can communicate with your guides in a way that is not mentioned here. There are many different ways of making contact. My friend who collects autumn leaves is the only person I have ever come across who makes contact that way. However, to her it is perfectly natural, and she receives the help and support that she needs using this method. It has never occurred to her to use a ouija board or a pendulum to make contact, as the way she discovered for herself works so well. You may find that one way is perfect for you, or you may prefer to use whichever method seems appropriate at the time. Experiment until you find a method that is comfortable for you.

Is It My Imagination?

Many people doubt the information that comes through from their spirit guides, thinking that "it is just" their imagination. Your imagination is limitless. The world as we know it today would not exist if people had not used their imaginations, thought of something, and then made it happen. Thomas Edison imagined the lightbulb and the phonograph before setting out to make them real. In fact, with the lightbulb he had more than 700 failures before achieving success. This says volumes about his determination and persistence, but the key to the whole exercise was his imagination. And how often do we say "it is just" our imagination!

You can travel anywhere in the universe in your imagination. You can go back and forth through time. Your imagination creates your reality. In other words, it creates your world. Much of the communication you receive from your guides may come through your imagination, but this does not make it any less real. Be open to anything your imagination tells you. It is a valuable means of communicating with your spirit guides.

The traditional methods of making contact with our spirit guides are all useful today. Michael, the famous channel who is the subject of *Messages from Michael* and *More Messages from Michael*,[23] originally came through a ouija board. He has since come through in a variety of other ways, including automatic writing. Jane Roberts originally found "Seth" through a ouija board.

Although they are all fun to use, they are not parlor games. Approach them in a lighthearted manner, but with serious intent, and they will serve you well.

13

Finding Spirit Guides Through Intuition

In my psychic development classes I found that many people were able to contact their spirit guides using intuition alone. In other words, they were able to sense, feel or even see their spirit guides, and did not need to use the traditional methods of automatic writing, table-tipping, ouija board, or pendulum.

My friend who psychometrizes autumn leaves is an example of someone who uses her intuition to communicate with her spirit guides. Most people who use intuition to contact their spirit guides either sense or see them.

Sensing Your Guides

You will need to find a comfortable place where you will not be disturbed while learning to sense your guides. I have a pleasant spot outdoors which I use during the summer. Naturally, I prefer to do this indoors when it is cool or wet. If you do it indoors, temporarily disconnect the phone and ask other members of the household not to disturb you. You may prefer to tell your family that you are going to meditate, rather than explain that you are contacting your guides. Both are correct, incidentally, as we use a form of meditation to sense our spirit guides.

Sit down or lie down comfortably. You may wish to cover yourself with a blanket, because many people lose a couple of degrees of body temperature while meditating.

Close your eyes and take yourself through a progressive relaxation exercise. It makes no difference how you do this, just as long as you allow yourself to relax totally. One method I particularly enjoy is to take a few deep breaths and then imagine myself standing on a bluff overlooking the beach and the ocean. There are ten steps leading down to the beach below and I double my relaxation with each breath I take. Consequently, by the time I reach the beach and lie down on the warm, enfolding sand I am totally relaxed.

Usually, at this point, I spend a few minutes trying to eliminate any negativity I may have built up in my body since the last time I did this exercise. We all think negative thoughts at times, and these can seriously affect our progress through life. For instance, a few years ago I suggested to someone who had extremely negative thoughts regarding money that he go through this process every time he contacted his guides. Over a period of time he was able to let go of this negativity and is now moving ahead financially.

I do not always have time to do this part of the exercise, but try to spend at least a few moments clearing any obstacles or obstructions that might be holding me back.

I rest for a few moments after this, savoring the anticipation of being in contact with one of my spirit guides. I allow myself to feel the warmth of the sand on my bare arms and legs. I feel the gentle breeze as it caresses my body. I listen to the seagulls and the sound of the waves breaking on the beach. I smell the clean, salty air. In effect, I am actually at the beach sensing and experiencing everything that I would feel if I were actually there. When this picture is so clear in my mind that I would feel a sense of shock if I opened my eyes and discovered I was not really lying on the beach, I am ready to contact my spirit guides. This is a state of relaxed awareness. I am totally relaxed physically, but at the same time I am extremely aware and sensitive mentally.

After a few moments I usually experience a tingling sensation in the small of my back. It rises up my spine and into my neck. This tells me that my guide is present.

You may experience something completely different. You might have a sudden sense of knowing that he or she is present, or perhaps you will experience a tingling sensation in your toes or fingers. You may suddenly feel a sense of warmth or security, similar to that wonderful feeling of being tucked in bed by your mother when you were very small. You may feel a gentle touch on your shoulder or some other part of your body. The response may be an emotional one, with great feelings welling up inside you. You may have an urge to laugh or cry, or do both together. You may feel a sensation of wonderful, ineffable love pervading every cell in your body.

It makes no difference what feelings or emotions you experience. You will suddenly become aware that your spirit guide is there with you, and it will be the most wonderful feeling in the world.

You may well experience this the very first time you go through this exercise. In my classes some thirty-five percent of the students managed to achieve this on their first attempt. The others had to practice this exercise a number of times before their guides came through.

It makes no difference ultimately if your guides appear on the first attempt or the hundredth. Once they do come through, you will be able to contact them in the future whenever you wish, so it is well worth whatever length of time it takes.

There can be any number of reasons guides do not appear on the first attempt. You might be tired, or stressed, or overly anxious. You may feel skeptical about the whole thing. You might feel that you should be busy doing something else, rather than relaxing quietly on your own.

Outside noises, such as a television set blaring in the next room, may affect the outcome.

Do not blame yourself if your guides do not appear immediately. Be patient, and simply try again and again until you achieve success. You will find the rewards will easily repay any amount of time spent on the exercise.

Seeing Your Guides

It is usually easier to see other people's guides than your own. It can be disconcerting the first time you see someone else's guide. It may appear as a flicker or shadow that has you wondering if you really did see anything. They can sometimes appear as a ball of color, a sound, or a smell. It may also be revealed as a perfect human form, possibly wearing unusual or outdated clothing. Often, guides appear to be identifiable figures such as Native Americans, Chinese sages, Ascended Masters, or a spiritual leader.

I always take it as a compliment to see someone else's spirit guide. It means that person's guide has enough confidence and trust in me to allow me to see him or her. Consequently, you must always treat other people's guides with love, care and respect, which is exactly the way they will treat you.

You may find that your spirit guide makes him or herself visible to you without your asking. There is likely to be a reason. Your guide may want to eliminate any doubts you have in your mind. He or she might want to bolster your confidence, or offer special support when it is needed.

Remember to be grateful when your guide does appear in this way. You are likely to be surprised and consequently neglect to say "thank you." Your spirit guides will forgive you for any lack of manners, but all the same, it is a good habit to regularly thank your spirit guides for any help they give you. We all like to be thanked for things that we have done, and your guides are no exception.

To see our own guides we need to develop the ability to see with our inner eyes. The easiest way is to use a mirror.

Buy a good-quality mirror. The size is not important, though I find one that is two feet high and one foot wide works well for me. Hang the mirror on the wall in a place where you are able to look directly at the center of it when you are sitting down in a comfortable chair.

Now you need a small round circle, approximately half an inch in diameter. I find a small office label works well for this. Attach this small dot to the mirror just above the center. In other words, when you are sitting down, you will need to look up very slightly to look at the circular dot on the mirror.

Finally, you need a large white candle. Light the candle and place it level with the bottom of the mirror on your left-hand side. Turn out the other lights in the room, and sit down in the chair. You should be able to see both the candle and its reflection in the mirror.

Relax and gaze at the small dot you have placed on your mirror. Remain as relaxed as you can, but keep staring at the circle with a direct, fixed gaze. After a while, your eyes will feel tired. Ignore this; it is simply a stage in the process.

Before long you will start to see things in the mirror. Do not shift your gaze to look at them. Keep on staring at the circle. Suddenly, the circular label will appear to vanish and you will see things clearly in the mirror.

You may or may not see your spirit guides. Sometimes, you will receive a clear message from them in the form of words that appear in the mirror. Sometimes you will see a scene as clearly as if it were actually taking place in front of you. And, sometimes, you will see your spirit guides.

The danger is that you will be so excited at seeing them that your gaze will change and the visions in the mirror will instantly disappear. If this happens, and it is very likely the first few times you do this, do not try to repeat the exercise again right away. It is better to leave it until the following night when you will be refreshed and ready to do it again.

Do not berate yourself when you start shifting your gaze and lose the picture. Even experienced people do it from time to time. It is natural to get caught up in the excitement of the experience and forget the importance of staying clearly focused on the one spot.

You will find your mirror an extremely practical and useful way of seeing your spirit guides. You will also find it useful for clairvoyance and precognition. In effect, used this way, the mirror acts much like a crystal ball. Predicting the future with a crystal ball is known as *scrying*, and can be done in many ways. I have seen people doing it with a drop of India ink, a thumbnail, a glass of water, or a mirror.

Do you remember the story of Snow White? Now you know the relevance of the words "Mirror, mirror on the wall." Mirrors have been considered magical objects for thousands of years.

Look after your mirror. Keep it clean and free of dust. Do not use it for mundane tasks, such as brushing your hair. Keep it for your special, magical purposes, and it will serve you well.

Making Direct Contact with Your Guides

All of the previous methods have helped many people get in touch with their spirit guides. I frequently use a pendulum or automatic writing, so I know from my own experience just how valuable and useful these techniques of the early spiritualists can be.

However, there will be times when you might wish to make direct contact with your guides, without the necessity for a ouija board, pendulum, table, or pen and paper. Fortunately, you can do this very easily.

Simply close your eyes and take three deep breaths, holding each breath for a few seconds before exhaling slowly. Allow yourself to relax as much as you can. This may not always be easy. For instance, if you are sitting at your desk at work, it might be hard to close your eyes for a few seconds, let alone become noticeably relaxed. With practice you will be able to do this exercise in a matter of seconds anywhere you happen to be. In time you will also be able to do it with your eyes open.

Do not practice this at work, at least not initially. You will find it much easier, and more successful, to experiment with this in bed at night, or perhaps sitting down in a comfortable chair.

After the deep breaths, forget about your breathing. The deep breaths will have served the purpose of putting extra oxygen into your brain and partially relaxing you. You will continue to breathe with steady, deep breaths, but there is no need to be conscious of this.

Become in tune with your inner self. Think pleasant thoughts and remain as still as possible. Become aware of any thoughts or feelings that come to you. It is important to think only pleasant thoughts, because your moods and feelings will be instantly picked up and responded to by the spirit world. Because you want to attract wealth, love, and happiness, rather than poverty, hate, and misery, it is important to think positively.

Try not to analyze the thoughts as they come into your conscious mind. Simply note them, and remain quiet and calm. These thoughts may or may not be coming from your spirit guides.

Fortunately, once you are in tune with your inner self, it is a simple matter to call on your guides. Say something like this to yourself: "I am ready and waiting. Please help me. I am ready to receive." If you have a specific problem that you are concerned about you can ask for help in resolving it. Usually, I have no particular problem in mind, but simply want to make contact for support and encouragement.

Once you have called on your guides, stay still and quiet and see what happens. You might feel a warmth around you. The response might be a gentle touch somewhere on your body. You might feel a sense of well-being and security. An acquaintance of mine gets a twitch in her little finger. Pay attention to everything that happens. Many times I felt that I had failed to make contact, only to realize later on that I had received a response but had not been aware of it.

You might have to do this several times before you become aware of any response from your guides. On the other hand, it may well happen the very first time you try.

A friend of mine was going through a marriage breakup when I suggested he try to make contact. To his amazement, he received an answer immediately, in the form of thoughts that arrived in his conscious mind. They made him aware of the reasons the relationship had foundered and what he should do to get his life back in order again. I had not expected him to experience such a dramatic first encounter with his spirit guides, but was grateful, as it enabled him to start his life anew.

Some people like to repeat a short saying over and over again when they are making contact with their guides in this way. I find this distracting myself, but mention it because many people find it helpful. They enjoy the repetition and find it helps them relax and become more in tune with their guides.

Many people panic when they first make contact using this method. There is no need for this. You are perfectly safe and can open your eyes any time you want. It is natural to feel nervous or timid, of course, but do not allow these feelings to ruin the spirit contact.

As soon as you feel any sort of contact, say silently, "Thank you." Your guides will receive this message and know that you are ready to meet them.

This is the time to ask any specific questions you may have. Simply think the questions to yourself. You may receive an answer immediately, but it could also take a number of days. No matter when the reply reaches you, always say, "Thank you." If the reply does not come straight away, repeat the exercise and ask the question again the following day, and each succeeding day until the reply arrives.

Even if you have no specific questions there will be things that you can ask about. See if you can learn your spirit guide's name. Ask about the other guides who are looking after you. Once you become familiar with communicating with your guides in this way you will become aware of any changes that occur.

A friend of my wife had always wanted to play a musical instrument but had never had the opportunity. A day or two after she had mentioned this to her guides, a neighbor offered her a flute, the very instrument she had been wanting to play. She found someone to teach her just as easily. Immediately after this, she noticed a difference in her spirit guides. She asked what was happening and discovered that she had two new guides who were there purely to help her progress musically. Obviously, her guides had enabled both the flute and the teacher to come to her, and then provided additional help with two musical guides.

Why were her guides so willing to help her learn a musical instrument? They were simply doing what all spirit guides do. They are there to help you, and will do all sorts of things behind the scenes to give you the right opportunities. However, it is still up to you to take advantage of them. This woman could easily have decided that she was too old, too busy, or too anything else to take up the flute, and then her guides would have let the matter rest. Because she seized the opportunity, they helped her find a teacher, and they will continue to help her develop her new skills just as long as she remains interested and prepared to do the work that is required.

This method of contacting your guides is a particularly useful one because, with practice, you will be able to do it almost instantly. That means that you can communicate with your guides while stuck in rush hour traffic, while taking a class, lying in the bath, waiting in line at the bank, or even while out enjoying a walk.

14

Spirit Guides and Emotional Health

As human beings, we lead lives ruled by our emotions. How many times have you said something while you were angry, and then later regretted your outburst? That is because our emotions always overrule logic. Of course, we can always apologize once we calm down, but we cannot take away the damaging words that we used, words that may well be remembered forever by the person to whom they were directed.

For a short while I lived with a person who suffered from feelings of jealousy. Although I have suffered from the effects of most emotions, jealousy has never been one, so this was a new experience for me. I was astounded to find that when she and her boyfriend went out together, he could not talk to another woman, because Mandy instantly became suspicious and jealous. She was also jealous whenever he went out by himself. She was jealous of a school friend's success in her career, jealous of other people at work—in fact, she seemed to be jealous of everyone. Consequently, she was leading a bitter, limited life, crippled by her own emotions. When her relationship broke up she finally went for counseling. The last time I saw her she was still plagued by her emotions, but at least was aware of the problem.

Mandy is an extreme case, of course. However, we all have problems with our emotions at times. Fortunately, with our spirit guides to help us, we are not alone. They are only too happy to help us overcome our limitations and become all that we can be.

Anger

Anger is the most common negative emotion, and we have all experienced it in varying degrees. It is interesting to note that some doctors believe that rage and anger can cause cancer, so people who are angry are probably doing as much harm to themselves as they are to others.

The next time you find yourself becoming angry, pause for a moment and take three deep breaths. If possible, drink a large glass of cold water as well. This pause serves two purposes. Stopping to take deep breaths enables us to fill our lungs and brains with oxygen. Naturally, it is vital to get oxygen into the brain, as when we are angry we often speak without thinking. Extra oxygen at this time can enable us to think more logically.

Secondly, a brief pause gives our spirit guides a chance to intervene. Listen to the small voice inside. Give it a chance to talk to you and you will find that it will counsel calmness and reason.

I was taught this lesson many years ago. I was taking a friend to the airport and we were running late. A car overtook us and then immediately slowed down to a crawl. I was furious. How dare he do that to me when I was already running late? I started yelling and punching the horn. My friend, who was the person trying to catch the flight, tapped me on the arm.

"Stop and think," he said. "You've allowed yourself to become angry because of what he did."

"He made me angry!" I retorted.

"No, he didn't. You let yourself become angry. You choose your own thoughts and emotions. No one can make you angry unless you let them."

I nodded because my friend was right. I drew back from the car in front and continued to the airport at a more sedate pace. My friend just managed to catch his flight, and I learned a valuable lesson.

I could have caused an accident by driving too close behind the car in front, or by trying to pass on a busy road. Anger would have clouded my thinking and I might have done something stupid. My friend, in effect, was my spirit guide that day. In fact, it may even have been my spirit guide who put the words into his mouth.

Just before we arrived at the airport, my friend told me a fascinating story about Buddha. Apparently, Buddha was speaking in a village square one day when one of the inhabitants started to abuse him. Buddha paused and said to the man: "If you offer me a piece of paper and I refuse to accept it, what happens to the paper?"

"Why, it stays with me, of course," the villager replied.

Buddha smiled gently. "And that is exactly what I am doing with your abuse," he said. "I am not accepting it. Therefore, it stays with you."

My spirit guide has given me advice in similar situations on numerous occasions since. By refusing to become angry, and pausing long enough for my spirit guide to come through with words of advice, I have been saved an enormous amount of emotional damage.

My spirit guide has given me a tremendous amount of advice concerning anger. He told me that if I had been born in the other person's body and had gone through the same upbringing and experiences that he or she had, I would be acting in exactly the same way. Once I realized this, many things that would have made me angry in the past did not affect me at all.

My guide also told me to pray for the people who make me angry. This seemed like terrible advice to begin with. However, once I thought it through, and remembered that thoughts contain energy and power, it made good sense. The people you pray for will immediately notice a difference in your attitude towards them, and the anger will be diffused on both sides.

The most important advice my guide gave me on anger was to ask me if the matter was worth getting angry over. At least ninety-nine percent of the time it isn't. Why waste valuable time and energy, and risk harm to yourself by becoming angry when there is no need for it?

Next time you find yourself becoming angry about something, pause and listen to your spirit guide. You will not regret it.

Envy

One of the Ten Commandments says: "Thou shalt not covet thy neighbor's house, thou shalt not covet thy neighbor's wife, nor his manservant, nor his maidservant, nor his ox, nor his ass, nor any thing that is thy neighbor's" (Exod. 20:17). Obviously, people have been envious of other people's successes and achievements for a long, long time!

An acquaintance of mine became very upset when a friend was promoted ahead of her at work. She was envious of her friend's new status, office, and income, and felt that she should have been promoted ahead of her friend.

Instead of pausing to think about the situation, she went to her boss and insisted that the promotion be rescinded. The outcome was that she lost both a friendship and her job.

Even then she could not stop thinking about the grave injustice she felt had been done to her. It was years before she finally realized that the promotion had been given to the right person.

"She worked harder than me, and had a better attitude towards the job," she told me with tears in her eyes. "Why couldn't I have seen that at the time?"

The reason she did not see it was because she was consumed with envy, and, as you know, emotions win over logic every time.

Greed

It is a natural desire to want more, but sometimes this can be taken too far. Greed can come out in many ways. Recently, I spoke with someone who had become estranged from her two brothers as they were contesting their mother's will in court. The brothers felt that they were entitled to a larger share of the estate than their sister. I have no idea of the rights and wrongs of this particular case, but the sister was convinced that her brothers were being greedy and unfair. If they were, they were obviously being far too greedy. Of what value is mere money if you are going to end up estranged from part of your family?

When I was a child I sometimes stayed at a friend's house for the weekend. We were good friends, but every time we sat down for a meal he would look at the amount of food on my plate and compare it to his. If he felt that I had been given a larger meal than his, he would complain loudly until his mother gave him more. "You're greedy!" she would say as she put more food on his plate.

It is interesting to note that he has not changed. He is just as greedy today as he was then. However, the greed now takes the form of getting more than his fair share out of the different businesses he is involved in. He is extremely well off financially, but I doubt that he is happy. He laughs when I remind him of his greediness at the meal table, but I doubt that he relates it in any way to his disastrous relationships with ex-wives and ex-business partners.

If you are tempted to want more than your fair share, pause and see what your spirit guide has to say. If you are short-changing yourself, your guide will certainly tell you. You can also be sure that your guide will let you know when you are being greedy.

Lust

Lust is an interesting emotion, as it can occur suddenly and unexpectedly. It also has enormous power and energy behind it. Consequently, most people find it hard to pause long enough to listen to their spirit guides.

When I was working with prison inmates I found that most of them regretted not waiting just a few seconds before acting. Many of them would not have been incarcerated if they had.

One way of handling lust is simply to observe its effects on your body. Do not fight it or act on it. Simply observe. The feelings of lust will diminish as you do this, and you will also be giving your spirit guides an opportunity to talk to you.

Stress

There is a saying that the only people who do not have stress are in graveyards. We need a certain amount of stress to function in life. However, there is good stress (eustress) and bad stress (distress). An athlete about to attempt a world record needs stress to perform at his very best. Most performers experience stress before they go on stage. This stress enables them to give better performances than they could otherwise achieve. The popularity of roller coasters and other seemingly dangerous rides at fairgrounds is due to the stresses that are experienced by the people enjoying the ride. Bungee jumping, parachuting, and other activities that contain an element of danger increase our stress levels. All of this is good stress.

However, stress caused by too much pressure at work, dysfunctional relationships, and too little time to do the things that need to be done can create health problems and even lead to an early death.

Too little stress can also kill. When I was growing up, a neighbor of ours retired. He had no hobbies or interests and died within eighteen months of giving up work.

The secret is to embrace good stress, as it adds happiness and stimulation to our lives, and to minimize bad stress. You may think this is impossible.

If you are working in an environment with a bad-tempered boss and constant pressure, it may seem a hopeless task to try to reduce the stress levels. However, with the help of your spirit guides you can relieve much of this stress.

If your boss appears and presents you with a large new task while you are in the midst of another job, you have a number of ways of handling it. You could simply sigh, accept the additional task, and increase your stress levels.

However, there are ways of handling the situation that do not affect your stress levels. You could always say "no," of course. However, this response would increase your boss' stress levels, and may make your job more unpleasant. Alternatively, you could say, "I'll get on to it as soon as I've finished this project." This lets your boss know that the task will be done, but that it might take some time. Another solution would be to say, "Shall I get on to that now, or would you rather I finished this job first?" All of these replies would reduce your stress levels.

Keep in touch with your spirit guides whenever you feel you are under too much stress. You can engage in a silent conversation with your guides, asking for help and advice.

Your guides might suggest that you say an emphatic "no" to a new task when you are already overworked. Your guides may well suggest a solution that you would not have thought of on your own. Listen to your guides and follow their advice.

Other Negative Emotions

Recognize that you are not your emotions. If you pause and observe your negative thoughts and feelings, you will become aware that they are coming from outside you. Therefore you have the power and control to let them in or to keep them out. What you decide to do is up to you, of course, but you must realize that you are damaging yourself by harboring negative emotions. Before allowing them in, pause and take a few deep breaths. Listen for your spirit guides. If you do not hear anything, invite your spirit guide in.

"I need your help," you might say. "Please advise me on how I should handle such-and-such a situation." Then carry on with whatever it was you were doing, and you will find your spirit guide will suddenly provide you with the answer you were seeking. It can often happen when you least expect it.

I remember becoming extremely upset about some matter many years ago. I cannot recall what it was now, but it seemed important at the time. While I was waiting for an answer from my guide, some friends called and suggested we go to a movie. I immediately cheered up and had a pleasant evening with my friends. Halfway through the film, my guide suddenly gave me the answer I wanted. I was amazed, as I had managed to forget all about my problem for a few hours. My spirit guide had deliberately waited until I was relaxed and calm before giving me the message I needed to hear.

Be patient. Ask your spirit guide for help and advice whenever you need it. You will always get an answer. Naturally, it may not be the answer you want or expect, but your spirit guide will always give you the answer that is right and fair to everyone concerned.

It is interesting to reflect that most emotional problems are caused by low self-esteem. Fortunately, our spirit guides can help raise our self-esteem, and this will be covered in the next chapter.

15

Greater Confidence and Self-Esteem

Several years ago I interviewed a man for a magazine article I was writing. He had overcome enormous difficulties and achieved great success. As a teenager he had belonged to a gang and several of his friends at that time were imprisoned for a variety of offenses.

"How did you manage to escape that sort of background unscathed," I asked him, "especially when some of your friends became hardened criminals?"

He shifted position in his chair and seemed uncertain whether to reply.

"You might find this hard to believe," he said. "But when I was very small, I had a teacher who really inspired me. She taught us about George Washington and what he did with his life. I've forgotten almost everything else I learned at school, but I can still recall virtually every word Mrs. Bagust said. She inspired me and for the first time in my life I wanted to know more. I learned everything I could about George Washington." He smiled and shook his head. "Why George Washington? Who can say? Anyway, one day we were fighting another gang and I was hurt. Just a minor stab wound, really, but I ended up in the hospital.

"The police wanted to know who had done it to me, but I wouldn't tell. The policeman left in disgust, telling me that I was a petty thug and would end up dead or else spend my life in jail.

"I thought about what he had said for a long time. I had nothing else to do. And then it suddenly came to me. What would George Washington have done in that situation? Well, he wouldn't have got himself involved with gangs in the first place. He would have fought fair, not the way we scrapped and brawled. I decided there and then that I'd model my life on George Washington. Every time I was about to do something I'd ask myself, 'Is this how George Washington would have done this?' I know it sounds strange, but it's George Washington who made me successful."

In fact, I did not find his words strange, as I had been doing something similar for many years. Instead of asking what George Washington would have done, I ask my spirit guide for help. Most of the time I receive a direct answer. When my guide fails to respond as quickly as I would like, I ask myself if what I was intending to do would make my spirit guide proud of me. If the answer is positive, I'll proceed to do it. I wish I could say that I never went ahead when the answer was negative. However, on the occasions I did proceed, despite receiving a negative answer, I always ended up regretting it. I have learned over the years that I make far fewer mistakes when I listen to my spirit guide and act in ways that would meet his approval.

A fascinating side benefit of this is that my confidence and self-esteem increased. Knowing that I had someone wiser and more knowledgeable than me to help and assist, any time I needed it, gave me much more assurance and a wonderful feeling of well-being.

You will find exactly the same thing occurring in your own life if you make constant, regular use of your spirit guide. That is what he or she is there for. Your spirit guide wants you to be confident and successful.

I talked about this at a drug rehabilitation center some years ago. About a year later I was stopped in the street by a young man who had been at the center at the time.

"You won't believe what's happened to me since you spoke," he told me. "I used to be stoned or drunk all the time. The rehab center dried me out, but I would have been straight back onto it again if you hadn't come. Nowadays, whenever I'm tempted, I ask my spirit guide if it is what I should do. He hasn't said 'yes' so far! I'll never go back now. You see, I have a job and a girlfriend."

He also has more confidence and self-esteem. He told me that he would never have come up and spoken to me in the past, because he would not have had the confidence to do so.

This is an example of someone who had spent most of his life ignoring the quiet voice of his spirit guide. Once he started to listen, his life turned around, and I am sure he is well on the way to a successful and fulfilling life.

Our spirit guides are there all the time working for us. However, many people who are usually aware of their guides have told me that they felt abandoned by their guides at the times they needed them most. In fact, this is not the case. Our spirit guides do not intrude and force themselves on us. They are there, whether we are aware of them or not. In fact, it is likely that your guides are working even harder for you than usual on these occasions. It is just that we sometimes fail to listen. Our guides are constantly encouraging us and trying to help us move ahead.

Most people say that they would like more confidence. However, most people also feel that they have good self-esteem. This is a contradiction because confidence comes as a direct result of feeling good about ourselves, which is good self-esteem.

I am sure that you can recognize the following indications of low self-esteem in yourself or in people you know: abusiveness, anger, co-dependency, cruelty, greed, impatience, jealousy, laziness, excessive materialism, moodiness, sarcasm, selfishness, shyness, and violence.

Do you know anyone who constantly puts down or abuses others; talks only about him or herself; interrupts others; intimidates others; complains about everything, or sulks when things do not go his or her way? This person is suffering from low self-esteem.

Recognizing low self-esteem is one thing. Correcting it and gaining a healthy, positive image of ourselves is another. It cannot be achieved overnight, but fortunately, with the help of our spirit guides, it can be done more quickly than you might expect.

First, we have to recognize what good self-esteem is. People who have healthy self-esteem have healthy egos. They feel good about themselves. They are warm, friendly, charismatic, and supportive of others. They have a sense of self-worth. They are positive and have a sense of being in control.

Most people are mixtures of high and low self-esteem. You will probably recognize traits of your own in both the low and high self-esteem areas.

How can we gain strong, healthy, high self-esteem? The answer is incredibly simple. We have to listen.

Constructive Listening

There are four different ways we have to listen. First, we must listen to other people. Really listen. Everyone has a story to tell, and we must learn to listen with interest and without interrupting. By doing this, we compliment the other person and raise his or her self-esteem. At the same time, we are increasing our own.

Secondly, we must listen to what is going on in the world around us. We must be alert for positive items in the media, and for true stories of heroism and how people overcame adversity. We attract whatever it is we think about, and by instilling these positive stories in our minds we gradually take on the positive attributes of the people we read about. Remember the man I interviewed who always asked himself what George Washington would do in any given situation? He gradually took on the positive attributes of this great man and achieved enormous success himself.

Thirdly, we need to listen to ourselves. Observe yourself in your different interactions with others. Are you exhibiting high or low self-esteem? Do not beat yourself up if you find yourself demonstrating low self-esteem. In other situations you will be revealing a good, high self-esteem. Simply resolve to do better next time when you find yourself revealing traits that you do not wish to have.

Finally, and most important, we must also listen to our spirit guides. Everywhere we go we take with us someone who wants us to do well, who is urging us on to success all the time. We need to pause and listen to what our spirit guides tell us. We may feel that our guides are taking away all our fun when they tell us not to do something that other people are doing. In fact, the advice our spirit guides provide will always be correct. Remember the prison inmates I spoke to? If they had listened, they would not be in jail right now. Your spirit guides will never give you advice that may hurt another living thing. Your guides are there to help and support you, but they also care for all life.

It is a wonderful fact that we have the power within us to change and become the people we were meant to be. Take one step at a time. Listen in the four different ways and prepare to take a quantum leap forward.

16

Your Limitless Guides

Last century, many mediums told their clients that they had forty-nine spirit guides. As you know, this was simply a ruse to keep people coming back. In fact, those mediums from a past age would be amazed at how many guides we actually do have. We have access to an unlimited number of guides who help us at different times in our lives. When you were a child your spirit guides may have been different from the guides you have now. We have the guides we need at different times and stages in our development.

However, we also have a limitless selection of guides who will come to our assistance at any time we ask them for help. If you are working on an artistic project you can call on a creative guide to help. You might ask a more practical guidc to assist you if you arc building a housc.

You might decide you want William Shakespeare to help you complete a certain project. You can call on anyone you wish, and he or she will be willing to help. Do not be disappointed with whomever comes through. William Shakespeare will certainly have many of the attributes of the Bard of Avon, but he will also be a composite of all the experiences he has had in many incarnations.

Specialist Guides

In practice, your guides want you to work independently and to make decisions for yourself. However, they are always willing to guide and help whenever required. Your own special guides are usually the best ones for day-to-day problems that occur. However, there will be times when you will want to consult with a specialist guide. The number and type of these are unlimited. Here are some of the main ones.

Intellectual Guide

When you are studying or engaged in research you may want the assistance of an intellectual guide. He or she can gently point you in the right direction to enable you to find the information you need.

This can happen in surprising or unusual ways. In the late 1960s I was living in London and doing research on the Celtic tradition. One day I was traveling on a double-decker bus. I generally stayed downstairs on these, as it was much easier to get off at the end of the ride. However, on this day, even though the downstairs was only partly filled, I went upstairs. On an empty seat was a copy of a book on Celtic mythology that I had not come across before. Someone must have left the bus, accidentally leaving the book behind. I made a note of the title, author, and publisher and was able to buy the book a few days later. If I had not, for some inexplicable reason, decided to go upstairs that day, I might never have found this particular book. Was this an accident, or had an intellectual guide gently encouraged me to go upstairs?

Wise Guide

A wise guide is not the same as an intellectual guide. A wise guide is someone who has gained knowledge and wisdom as he or she passed through life, possibly through numerous incarnations, and is prepared to pass that insight on when it is asked for.

A wise guide is particularly useful when you are faced with a major decision that could change your entire life. When you decide to marry someone you are making a decision that will change your life forever. The same thing applies if you are offered a job in another country, far away from home, friends, and family.

In these situations it is a good idea to ask a wise guide if the decision you intend to make is, in fact, a good one.

Naturally, emotional decisions are the hardest ones. If you ask a wise guide if you should marry someone and the guide says "no," but your heart says "yes," what should you do? The wise guide would not have given a negative answer without good reason. You might be taken aback by the answer. Think carefully, and then ask more questions. Why is the wise guide against the marriage? The answers might surprise you. Listen carefully and then think about the situation for a few days. If you are able to look at the situation dispassionately, you will find that the wise guide is right.

I have met a number of people who ignored the advice of their wise guides and suffered as a result. All your guides work for your best interests and will never give you bad advice. Neither will they interfere when you ignore their suggestions. You are here on this earthly plane to learn and grow. One of the best ways to learn is to make mistakes. Consequently, think carefully before asking your wise guides for assistance. It is better to approach them with the attitude that you will take their advice, no matter what it is, than to ask for help and then ignore it.

Practical Guide

I am not a handyman. I discovered years ago that if any repairs needed to be done around the house it was generally cheaper for me to employ a tradesman, rather than try to do the task myself. If you are a practical person, you probably also have a practical spirit guide. However, if you are like me in this regard, you can always call on a practical guide for assistance when you need it.

Some years ago I was surprised to hear that a friend had built a small sailing boat. This friend had never shown any signs of being practical with his hands before, but one winter he built the boat in his spare time. He told me that the urge to build the boat had gradually welled up inside him. He fought the desire for as long as he could, but one day found himself buying plans and tools.

The actual making of the boat went smoothly. "It felt as if someone was helping me every step of the way," he told me. "I instinctively knew which tools to use. My wife thought I'd cut off my fingers, but I seemed to know how to handle everything. It was a most enjoyable, relaxing experience."

My friend has not yet built anything else, but is considering a number of projects. How could this man, with no previous experience, successfully build a sailing boat? My friend is skeptical, but I am convinced that a practical guide helped him.

Remember, if your car breaks down miles from anywhere, to call on a practical guide for help. This guide may well lead your fingers to the problem area.

Creative Guide

Creativity can come out in many unexpected ways. Recently, I attended an exhibition of paintings by prison inmates. None of them had ever painted seriously before, yet the standard was extremely high. Admittedly, they had plenty of time to develop their skills in prison, but they had received very little in the way of tuition. Obviously, they were receiving help and encouragement from another source—creative guides.

In chapter 13 I mentioned a friend who was learning to play the flute. She had two creative guides waiting to help her before she requested their assistance. Ask for a creative guide to help you any time you are engaged in artistic or creative work.

Motivation Guide

We all need motivation and encouragement at times. When I was first thinking about leaving the security of a satisfying, well-paying job and becoming self-employed, my family and friends all urged me to stay where I was. They were thinking of me, of course. They did not want me to take unnecessary risks and do something that might have ended in failure.

However, we all need to take chances sometimes and get out of our comfort zones. If we didn't stick our necks out every now and again life would become dull and boring. I would hate to end up as an old man filled with regrets for the things I was too scared to do.

If you are ready to take a chance and do something new or different, ask your motivation guides for help. They will provide you with the necessary encouragement that you need. However, they will not encourage you to take crazy risks. They will also counsel caution when it is needed.

Loving Guide

Our guides are caring, non-judgmental, and concerned. They have our well-being at heart, even though they may sometimes appear slightly detached. This is deliberate, as they want us to stand on our own two feet and achieve independence for ourselves.

However, there are times when we need to feel loved and protected. If you are lonely, stressed, or depressed, a loving spirit guide can help enormously.

A loving guide can also help us when we are feeling our way into a new relationship. Daryl, a friend of mine in Australia, was finding it hard to express his love and devotion to his girlfriend, Jenny. He had gone through a difficult divorce and was terrified that Jenny would reject him. I suggested that he call on loving guides to help him say the right words.

The results far exceeded his expectations. "For the first time in my life," he told me, "I can say 'I love you' without the words sticking in my throat. They're simple words, but in the past I could never get them out. Now, I can't believe what I'm saying! I'm saying all the things I want to say but wasn't able to in the past."

Fun Guide

It may sound strange to hear of a "fun guide," but there are guides for every possible purpose. Many of us are inclined to take life too seriously. We seldom laugh or take time out for simple pleasures. If you feel that you are spending too much time at work and too little at play, call on a fun guide to help you relax and start to enjoy the small, fun things in life again. It will do you and your loved ones the world of good.

Recently, I spoke to a man who spent more than eighty hours every week working at his business. "How do your wife and family put up with those hours?" I asked.

"They like the money I bring home," he answered.

I am sure that if this man took more time off from his work and spent it with his family, they would all be much richer than they are now.

Some people actually forget how to have fun. Everything is serious and life is a grim business. Yet, when they were children they would have laughed and played with their friends. They had the ability then, but somehow lost it as they went through life.

When was the last time you spent quality time with your loved ones? When was the last time you laughed so much that it hurt? If it has been too long, call on your fun guides. They are always ready and willing to help.

Child Guide

Child guides usually prefer to work with children. These are the "invisible friends" so many of us had when we were young. Unfortunately, rather than encouraging this, our educational system usually manages to eliminate these invisible friends from our lives.

However, even as adults, we can contact child guides. If you are having problems with a child you might call on a child guide to offer advice on handling the situation. You might also call on a child guide and ask if he or she could take a special interest in the child you are concerned about.

A friend of mine had an extremely difficult childhood. Her parents separated when she was four years old and her mother became an alcoholic. She was alternately spoiled and abused throughout her childhood. When she was fifteen she ran away from home and did not contact either of her parents for several years. Now, in her early forties, she is happily married with a family of her own.

"I feel I missed out," she told me. "I see my kids playing and having fun, and then I think about my own childhood. I didn't really have one." She has a child guide who is helping her to remember the happy times from her childhood and to let go of all the sad and difficult times.

"Of course there were some happy times in my childhood," she says. "I'm gradually bringing them back, and at the same time I'm letting go of the hurt and pain." It is obviously working, as she is looking years younger than she used to, and is becoming a much happier, more contented person.

Companion Guide

When I was twenty-one the company I worked for transferred me to Glasgow. I knew no one there, and expected to feel lonely. When I arrived at Glasgow Railway Station a porter came up to me and I could not understand a single word he said! For a while it felt as if I were in a country where everyone spoke a different language. However, after a few days I suddenly became attuned to the Glasgow accent and everything seemed brighter. It still took me a while to meet people and make friends, but I was never lonely. I felt as if I had an invisible companion with me everywhere I went. This companion stayed with me until I made friends, and then quietly disappeared.

If you are feeling lonely or simply need someone to talk to, call on a companion guide. You must not use your companion guide in place of a real friend, though. Your spirit guides want you to be happy and to function well in this world. They will provide companionship for you whenever you need it, but they do not want to take the place of real, living friends.

Support Guide

Our spirit guides support us to the best of their ability. You can ask them whenever you need help and support. However, you may experience a situation where you need more than the usual amount of help. This is when you need to contact a support guide.

Monique is an attractive woman in her middle thirties. She was happily married with three children. Bob, her husband, was doing well in his career and was an excellent provider. Everything seemed to be just about perfect.

One day Jason, their seven-year-old son, was playing ball in their front garden with a friend. He raced out of the garden to catch the ball and was run over by a passing car. If it had not been for the speed and competence of the paramedics in getting him to hospital he would have died. As it was, he spent seven weeks in a coma hovering near death.

Monique spent that entire time by his side. Later, she told friends that she called on extra support to help her during that time. Her support guides helped her through the ordeal. They also helped her later when she and Bob learned that Jason would always walk with a limp.

Monique was helped enormously by her close-knit family and a wide circle of friends. However, her support guides gave her extra help when she needed it desperately. If you find yourself in a situation where you need all the extra help and support you can muster, do not forget to call on your support guides.

Nurturing Guide

Nurturing guides help us when we need extra support for something we are working on. If you are an athlete training for a special event, your nurturing guide can keep you motivated and clearly focused on your goal.

A keen gardener I know decided one year that he was going to win the prize for growing the largest pumpkin in a county fair. His nurturing guide helped him by offering support and even giving advice on what to feed the plant. A large photograph of the prize-winning pumpkin is now displayed in his living room.

No matter what it is you are working on, if it requires extra help over a period of time, remember to call on your nurturing guides.

Healing Guide

I believe that we all have healing gifts and can heal both ourselves and others. With some people this quality is more evident in their makeup than in others, but we all possess it. We can use healing guides to increase our healing capabilities.

If someone you know is ill, send a healing guide to help. Sit down quietly somewhere, relax, and visualize a healing guide healing your friend. Send healing thoughts as well. Do this at least once a day until your friend is completely well again.

You can use guides to help heal yourself as well. If you feel unwell, imagine a healing guide surrounding you with energy and filling you with vibrant health and vitality. Keep on doing this until your health is fully restored.

Not long ago at a lecture, a woman asked me whether these limitless guides were in fact limitless in number. "Your guide can change shape and appearance any time it wants," she said. "Surely all these other guides are simply your own personal guide changing shape and identity to suit the situation."

It was a good question, and one I've thought about a great deal since. To the best of my knowledge, these guides are additional guides that come to our aid when called upon. I distinctly remember during my first few weeks in Scotland that I had a companion guide as well as my usual guide. My usual guide did not transform itself into a companion guide, but since I had not consciously requested a companion guide, I assume that my spirit guide summoned it for me, realizing I needed a companion.

As the spirit world is made up of thought forms, you can call on any form of guide that you feel the need for at any time. For instance, if you are thinking about taking up a certain sport or creative activity, you can call on a spirit guide who is knowledgeable on the subject.

A friend of mine wanted to turn her hobby of acting into a full-time career. Everyone was against it, especially her parents, but she asked for a guide who would help her start in the right direction and keep her on track. Several years later she is doing well in her chosen field and her parents are her biggest fans. If she had not called on a special guide to help her, she would probably still be a bank teller.

It is wonderfully reassuring to know that these special guides are there, ready and waiting for us, whenever we need them. All you need do is ask.

17

Psychic Circle

Like-minded people tend to attract each other. It is natural for people with similar interests to want to spend time together discussing whatever topics they have in common. Consequently, you are likely to come into contact with other people who are interested in spiritual growth. You can learn a great deal from other people, and they in turn will learn from you. Some of them will be more advanced in their spiritual quest than you, but others will be just starting on their search.

You might find it helpful to suggest to these like-minded people that you start a small, informal group to discuss spiritual matters on a regular basis. You will be able to practice things, such as automatic writing, together in a safe, secure environment. You will be able to share books and take part in tests and experiments that you might not be able to do on your own. You will also find that group sittings help encourage spirit contact.

The members of the group will find it much easier to make contact with their spirit guides as part of the circle, rather than on their own. The energy that a group can put out is much stronger and more vibrant than someone working on his or her own. This makes spirit contact easier to achieve, and also puts at ease the minds of those members who might be a bit nervous about contacting spirit guides.

The most useful thing I have noticed in these groups is that everyone develops their talents much more quickly. Many people, even today, are afraid to talk about their interest in these subjects. Consequently, although they may read about it, they seldom get an opportunity to discuss it or to try to develop further. When I first left school I worked with someone for several years and had no idea that he was interested in the psychic world. It was only years later, when our paths crossed at a psychic convention, that we realized we had an important interest in common.

I think it is important to keep the group, or circle, reasonably small and informal. Once the group gets too large, politics seems to creep in, and before you know where you are you are spending half of your time in formal business meetings with little time left for developing spiritually.

One group I belonged to was completely destroyed over a period of time by one member who was jealous of the abilities of other members and used a variety of underhanded methods to force them out. When they resigned, many of the other good members also left, and the group disintegrated.

Keep your group small and think carefully before inviting anyone new in. It makes no difference if all your members are at a different stage of development. The ones who are more advanced or knowledgeable will help the others grow.

You might design a formal curriculum or you might choose to play it by ear and see how it develops. It is a good idea to invite guest speakers in on a regular basis. Their ideas can help the group grow and provide useful topics for discussion later.

If you are the one putting the group together, make a list of the things that you want included. A few weeks ago I spoke to a group of ten teenagers who have a very active circle. The leader of this group is a seventeen-year-old high school senior. When she started the group she had very strict ideas on what would and would not be allowed.

For instance, no one was allowed to smoke at the meetings. Drugs were also forbidden, of course. She also would not allow anyone in whom she considered to be either a sexist or a bully. She arranged for the members to take turns providing supper after the meetings. The supper was excellent on the night I spoke to them, and she told me it was always that good, as she insisted on it. None of these things have anything to do with psychic development, but because she founded the group and laid down the ground rules, she put them in place, and now they are a natural part of the way in which the circle functions.

Arrange for the meetings to be held at a regular place and time. An hour or two a week is probably enough. If you meet just once a month, interest can die, and someone who misses a meeting for some reason has to wait two months before being able to attend again.

Do not make the meetings too long. Most people are busy, and not everyone can afford to spend three or four hours a week attending a spiritual group. If you meet at a regular time and place every week, your spirit guides will know and be ready and waiting for you to arrive.

Ensure that the meetings are fun. Use music, singing, candles, incense and colored lights. Encourage jokes and laughter. Contacting your spirit guides does not have to be a serious, heavy business. Your spirit guides will appreciate the lighthearted atmosphere as much as everyone else. In fact, you will find that many of them have an excellent sense of humor and will surprise you with their jokes and witticisms.

Vary your program. One week everyone might try automatic writing. Next week, you might conduct a séance, and the week after have a discussion and demonstration of psychometry. You might want to start and finish the same way each week, possibly with a song or prayer, but change the format regularly.

One group I speak to every now and again has a surprise speaker one evening every month. Only the organizer knows who will be invited, so no one knows the speaker or the topic until they arrive. This group has found that it keeps members' interest high. No one wants to miss a meeting in case it turns out to be an especially good one!

If your group is small, you can meet around a table. If the group is too large for this, arrange the chairs in a circle. This is more friendly than having the chairs arranged in rows facing the organizer, which is reminiscent of school days. It is better if any socializing, before or after the meeting, is done in another room. That way, one room is kept specifically for spiritual contact. This is not always possible, of course. If you do not have access to another room, ensure that any socializing is done after the meeting, rather than before.

Appoint a record keeper. Again, you might wish to have your members take turns in doing this. As soon as the session is over, this person has to write down what happened. This provides a permanent record of the event and can often help clarify and provide further insight into the spirit messages.

Incidentally, I also make my own record of the evening once I get back home. This is done for my own benefit. I record everything that I can remember, but naturally, the emphasis of my personal report is on matters that pertain to me. I find that doing this often clears up any confusion I may have experienced. If you do this, you will find that over a period of time you will build up a valuable record of your spiritual progress.

Suggested Meeting Format

1. Everyone gathers in another room and then enters the spirit room together. Latecomers dissipate the built-up psychic energy. You may wish to have a policy of not allowing latecomers in until there is a natural pause in the proceedings.

2. Everyone sits down. Make sure that people do not sit in the same place every week, or always sit beside their friends. Move people around and make sure that everyone gets to know everyone else.

3. When everyone is seated, begin with a ritual of some sort. You might start by having everyone hold hands while you say a prayer or an invocation. It might be a good idea to have a different person say the prayer each week. It is good to get everyone involved. You might sing one or two hymns or spiritual songs. You might have a small ceremony in which music is played while four candles are lit, one in each of the four major directions.

4. A brief meditation would be in order here to help everyone relax. You might have everyone close their

eyes and take part in a progressive relaxation to allow everyone to become inwardly as quiet as possible.

5. Dim the lights and allow everyone to meditate quietly on their own for a couple of minutes. Encourage people to talk about what they see, sense or feel at this time. Some people, for instance, might see spirit lights or feel a change in the temperature of the room. They might feel a presence near them, or receive an intuitive insight that they wish to share. This part of the evening can be extremely valuable for everyone present.

6. Depending on how long the group has been meeting, one or more people will receive messages from their spirit guides. Allow these people time to speak. As each week passes, more and more people will make contact with their spirit guides, so this part of the evening will gradually lengthen. Remember that you might receive a message for someone else in the group. You may also entertain spirits who come for just one or two meetings and never reappear.

   Not everyone will want to share. Respect this. On the other hand, some people want to give their entire life histories to the group every week. Speak to these people quietly after the meeting. You do not want to discourage them, but point out that this part of the evening is for everyone to have an opportunity to share.

7. As the facilitator, you need to maintain a balance between making contact with your own spirit guide and ensuring that the meeting runs smoothly and successfully. For instance, you might want to put on music or have everyone sing a song if you feel that the energy is flagging. At one group I attended, the facilitator had everyone stand up and do some stretching exercises halfway through the evening. Instead of disrupting the proceedings, it helped everyone relax further and created a perfect atmosphere for spirit communication.

8. To conclude, play meditation music, offer a prayer of thanks, and sing a cheerful song. Finish the evening with supper, preferably in another room. Naturally, people will want to talk about what has been accomplished, but encourage them to talk about other aspects of their lives as well. It is important that you all get to know each other as real people, rather than as faces you see across a table once a week.

You will find that in time the room where you hold these meetings will develop an atmosphere of its own. Your regular attendees will feel it every time they come in, and will immediately feel relaxed. This special atmosphere helps establish the right mood for the evening and raises everyone's expectations.

Sometimes you will have specific questions you want to ask your spirit guides. Make sure that you ask them as part of a group. Sometimes you may want to ask certain questions privately, on your own. On other occasions, you may have no questions at all and be content to see what happens.

Rather than forming your own group, you may wish to join an existing one. This is an excellent way of meeting a number of like-minded people at one time and if you find that you fit in well with the group, join it. If you find it is not right for you, attend other groups until you find one that you like. Every circle has its own different way of doing things, and you may have to compromise a little bit.

You may prefer to develop on your own. That's fine, too. The energy of a group is strong and powerful and often makes for quicker progress, but if you are in a situation where it is not practical to join a group, or you simply do not want to, it is perfectly all right to do it on your own. The well-known psychic, Tudor Pole, frequently said: "Every man his own medium."[1] (Today I'm sure he would say, "Every person his or her own medium.")

You need to be reasonably well disciplined to do it on your own. Set aside a certain amount of time every week for contacting your spirit guides. Make a ceremony or ritual of it if you wish. Lighting candles or burning incense is a good way of creating the right atmosphere. Rather than singing hymns out loud, you might prefer to read an appropriate passage from a book silently. It makes no difference where you hold your weekly session with yourself, but make sure it is a place where you are unlikely to be disturbed.

Whether you choose to do it on your own, or in a group, your spiritual circle will help you make contact with your spirit guides.

Séances

The meetings of your psychic circles are, strictly speaking, séances, as the intent is to communicate with your spirit guides. The popular conception of a séance is quite different. People imagine sitting in a darkened room, holding hands while a variety of strange things occur. They expect to hear strange sounds, or perhaps see a ghost or floating trumpet. They especially hope to communicate with someone, usually a dead relative or a celebrity, such as Marilyn Monroe or Elvis Presley. They expect to see strange props, such as a spirit trumpet or ouija board.

In reality, a séance is usually more like the psychic circle meetings. This wasn't always the case. In the 1880s, when spiritualism was at its height of popularity, thousands of séances were being held every week across the United States. Many of these were fraudulent, but they were invariably great entertainment in pre-radio and television days.

The mediums used a variety of ruses to keep people coming back. One of these was to tell the sitters that they each had seven bands of seven spirit guides. Consequently, the sitter had to return at least forty-nine times to learn the names of all of his or her spirit guides.

The first spirit guide to make an appearance at one of these séances would be the medium's guide, usually referred to as the "control." Now as then, the first personal spirit guide a sitter meets is his or her "Joy Guide." This is usually a small child who is warm, caring, and "all-knowing." This comes from Matthew 18:3 in the Bible, in which Jesus told his disciples: "Verily I say unto you, Except ye be converted, and become as little children, ye shall not enter into the kingdom of heaven." The medium's control is often his or her Joy Guide.

Other popular guides at nineteenth-century séances included: "Indian," who looked after the environment and found lost objects; "Medical Doctor," who gave health and medical advice; "Chemist," who advised on nutrition; "Doctor of Philosophy," source of personal advice and counsel; "Nun" or "Saint," who had been martyred for the sitters; and "Master Teacher," a very old, wise person. It was a highly auspicious day when the Master Teacher visited the séance room.[2]

Although these mediums were undoubtedly taking advantage of the credulous, it appears there is an unlimited variety of different guides. For instance, an intellectual guide will help you grow academically. A loving guide will help you find the right person to share your life with. An astute businessman I know has a guide who helps him make complicated investment decisions. In actuality, there are considerably more than forty-nine guides to choose from.

In most of the séances held in the golden age of spiritualism, the voices would come through a spirit trumpet that appeared to float in the air and move around the room. After every sitter had received a message, the trumpet would drop to the floor, marking the end of the séance.

The spirit trumpets would also produce *apports*. These are gifts from the spirits, and take a number of forms. Sometimes they are small trinkets, but can also be shells, flowers, coins, fossils, and even items that the sitters have previously mislaid. In the dark the sound of the apports arriving through the trumpet is strange and exciting, as you do not know who the apport will be for. The sound is much like that of a coin going around and around as it heads down a spiral. Many of the wishing wells that you find in today's shopping malls operate in this way.

Sometimes apports simply appear. At one séance I attended, the table was sprinkled with autumn leaves when the lights were turned on. The strange thing was that I attended the séance in spring!

In some nineteenth-century séances every sitter received a coin that dropped into their hands from the trumpet. When the lights were turned on, they would discover that they had each received a coin minted in the year they were born!

Many of the séances in these halcyon days of spiritualism included the materialization of a spirit from a spirit cabinet. This cabinet was often a corner of the room with a black cloth acting as a screen and curtain. The medium would enter the cabinet, and an assistant would explain that the medium was going into trance to allow the ectoplasm to build up in the room. After a prayer and a hymn, the sitters would be advised to keep their feet on the floor and their hands palm-upwards in their laps. Then, assuming everything went well, a materialization would appear, either from inside the cabinet or from the center of the room.

Unfortunately, many mediums resorted to trickery and virtually discredited spiritualism. At the turn of the century it was estimated that half of the American population were spiritualists.[3] What percentage do you imagine are spiritualists today? That demonstrates the dramatic fall in popularity that spiritualism suffered.

Unfortunately, the activities of the fake mediums allowed skeptics to say that all mediums were frauds, when this is far from being the case.

Drop-In Communicators

Every now and again at a séance you will receive a message from a spirit that does not relate to anyone present in the room. These spirits are called "drop-in communicators." Obviously, these spirits want to make contact with their loved ones, but are finding it hard to do so. I find them particularly fascinating because they eliminate any possibility of fraud or deception.

About twenty years ago I was participating in a séance when the medium's voice suddenly lowered an octave and in a man's voice she said: "Please help me. Died August 8, Chicago. Mechanic. Slight stutter."

The medium then carried on with messages for other people in the group. Afterwards, when we were discussing what came through, we found that no one related to the message from the mechanic. However, a week later, at the next séance, he came through again, telling us his name was John Campbell and he wanted his family to know that he was happier than he had ever been while alive.

One of the people present volunteered to check out the death notices to see if anyone by that name had died on August 8 in any of the last few years. This was a more difficult task than we had assumed. Chicago covers a huge area and the main papers did not include everyone who died in the outlying suburbs.

Over the next few weeks, more information came through from John Campbell. Apparently, he had never married, though he was engaged at the time of his death. He appeared to be keen on motor racing, and his ambition in life was to become a professional racing driver. He was working as a mechanic when he died, so evidently he did not achieve that goal. He died as a result of a car accident when he misjudged a corner. This sad story entranced everyone in the group, and we all spent time trying to locate his family in the hope of passing on the message and learning more about his life.

We found several John Campbells who had died close to August 8, but none of them had been mechanics. We also located another John Campbell who was born on that day and had been a mechanic. However, he had been married with a family.

John Campbell came through several times and then stopped visiting. The medium tried to make contact, but with no success. Sadly, we were never able to verify the story.

Drop-in communicators have been a lifelong study for Dr. Alan Gauld, a senior lecturer in psychology at Nottingham

University. He became interested in the subject while a student at Cambridge University in the late 1950s. He joined a circle which had been established during World War II and lasted until 1964. Fortunately, the couple who organized it kept excellent records.

These were passed on to Alan Gauld, who began investigating them. Some 240 spirits had come through the ouija board and, not surprisingly, most were relatives of the sitters. However, there were also thirty-eight drop-in communicators. Thirteen of these gave so little information that they could not be verified. A further fifteen also could not be verified, because the information they gave does not match the historical records. John Campbell, who came through at the séances I attended, is another example of this. However, Dr. Gauld was able to check out and verify ten communicators.

In each case he ensured that the spirit was not in any way connected with any of the sitters. He also researched birth, death, and marriage certificates, and other printed records. He compared details given at the séances to information provided by the surviving relatives and friends. Finally, he had to make sure that the sitters had not learned the information accidentally, perhaps by reading about it in a local newspaper or magazine.[4] When you hold your own séances, pay attention to any drop-in communicators, as they may provide compelling evidence for life on the other side.

The Dark Séance

You may wish to experiment with a traditional dark séance. Make sure that you choose honorable, honest people to participate. It is much better to conduct a séance with four people you can trust implicitly, than to hold an impressive séance with a dozen or more people, and wonder whether someone was cheating in the dark.

In fact, even with people you trust it is better to have some light in the room. A fifteen-watt red lightbulb produces sufficient light to allow everyone to see what is going on, and seems to aid concentration.

Most large séances are held with the sitters arranged in a circle or horseshoe arrangement. A table to hold any essential items is on one side. With just a handful of people, it is better to sit around the table. Everyone should hold hands with the people on either side and preferably have their feet touching as well.

It is important that you go into the séance with a specific aim in mind. Most people who take part in dark séances want a physical manifestation of some kind. This can occur, but is less common than people seem to think. It is most unlikely to happen the first few times you attempt it. You need to be patient.

You may wish to start by placing a compass in the center of the table and have the group concentrate on having the needle move to a particular position. Once it has done that, ask one person to leave the table and see if the compass will still move without the concentration of the missing person.

If it can, ask another person to leave the table. Keep on doing this until the needle in the compass will not move.

Do this experiment again, but ask different people to leave the table this time. By the time you have done this several times you will have a clear indication of which people in the group have the most latent ability.

Spirit photography can also prove useful, and Polaroid photographs mean that the results can be assessed instantly. To do this effectively, one person stays outside the circle and acts as the official photographer. The other sitters concentrate on making contact with their spirit guides. The photographer should take a photograph every five minutes or so, taking each photograph from a different position.

You may be fortunate enough to obtain a photograph of a spirit. It is more likely that you will find flashes of light or clouds of vapor in these photographs.

Spirit photography dates back to 1861, when William Mumler of Boston accidentally photographed the spirit of his dead cousin while trying to take a photograph of himself. When he repeated the experiment he found other spirits had joined his cousin in the picture. Word soon spread, and Mumler gave up his job and became a full-time spirit photographer.

Keep a record of every séance, even when nothing seems to have occurred. You may find a gradual picture building up to reveal steady progress, even when you might have felt you were standing still. This can be highly encouraging.

It is also worth keeping a record for posterity. If the couple who kept records of every séance for twenty years had not done so, Dr. Gauld would never have been able to verify the accounts of the drop-in communicators.

Visiting a Medium

You may decide that you would like to make contact with your spirit guides by having a sitting with a medium. You will find it an interesting experience. Most of the people who visit mediums are grieving relatives who want to make contact with deceased loved ones.

The hardest part of the exercise is to find a good medium. Ask like-minded people whether they know of anyone they could recommend. If this provides no leads, see if there is a spiritualist church near you and ask them for assistance. Unfortunately, there no longer seems to be a national organization of spiritualist churches in either the United States or Great Britain. However, contacts for many of the spiritualist churches in both countries can be found on the Internet.

Provide as little information as possible when making an appointment. You may even wish to use a pseudonym to preserve your anonymity until you arrive. This protects both you and the medium. If something personal and evidential comes through during the sitting, the medium would not want to be accused of reading the local obituary notices or doing other research. You are also protected, as you will know that anything relevant that comes through is genuine.

During the sitting itself, you naturally need to cooperate with the medium, but keep your answers to any questions as brief as possible. You do not want to influence the medium inadvertently. Some people chat away happily to the medium and unwittingly provide a vast amount of information. The medium does not want or need this, so be pleasant but brief.

If possible, tape the sitting for future use. Some mediums do not allow their sessions to be recorded, but it makes excellent confirmation of anything that comes through.

Do not expect miracles when trying to contact deceased relatives. A common complaint is that mediums provide trivial information. This is generally true, but tucked away in the midst of it all is often something of real value. I find it a good idea to have a prepared list of questions to ask. Otherwise, I would later think of a question I wished I had asked.

It is certainly not necessary for your progress to have a sitting with a medium, but I am sure you would find it interesting and, hopefully, evidential.

18

Becoming a Medium

A medium is a person who is able to act as the mouthpiece for departed spirits. He or she is able to communicate with other people's spirit guides and provide them with messages from the other side.

Some people become mediums naturally, while others are more reluctant. It is one thing to communicate privately with your own spirit guides, but it is quite another to communicate publicly with other people's guides. Many mediums communicate while in a trance state, and some people find it embarrassing at first to allow this to happen when other people are present.

Doris Stokes was one person who became a medium naturally. All her life she experienced voices talking to her and she found that by retelling what the voices told her she could help many others. She began communicating to friends in her kitchen, but the meetings grew larger and larger. Finally, when the weekly meetings filled her house, with people crammed into the hallway and up the stairs, she began holding her meetings in halls and churches.[1] Ultimately, she became known around the world for her gifts at communicating with the spirits.

Doris Stokes began with supportive friends. This is by far the best way to start. You will feel more comfortable and relaxed surrounded by people who believe in you and care for you than you will starting with a room full of strangers.

Where to Start

You may find it helpful to start within your development circle. This is particularly the case if your family is skeptical about your mediumistic abilities. It is much better to start with people who believe in what you are doing. You will pick up the negativity from the skeptics soon enough, and it is better to gain some confidence before facing that.

My friend, Pat Page, began her career as a professional medium at a service club. She had been invited as the guest speaker, but was introduced as a medium. Consequently, she felt that she had to include some spirit communication in her address. It turned out to be a total disaster. The group she was addressing was made up of hard-nosed business people with no interest in the spirit world.

"I could feel the skepticism as soon as I began," she remembers. "I was nervous enough, anyway, and that just made it worse. Fortunately, I can remember hardly anything about that evening."

In fact, that evening almost ended her career before it began. It was two years before she was brave enough to try again. The next time she did it with a group of friends and supporters and had no problems at all.

"Nowadays, I can handle the skepticism," Pat says. "In fact, I almost enjoy it as it keeps me on my toes. But to begin with, it was so overpowering. It was like a huge black cloud that came down and smothered me. I hate negativity, anyway, and try to mix with positive people. My favorite audiences are people who are open-minded. I don't care if they believe or not, just as long as they're prepared to be open and receptive."

Another friend of mine has not yet told his wife that he is a medium. He travels widely in the course of his work as a salesman, and regularly works as a medium in the towns and cities he visits. However, in his home town he tries to conform to his wife's ideal of a husband, and the fact that he is a gifted medium is not known by anyone. This has been going on for several years now, and he is feeling increasingly stifled by the situation.

"I'd love to tell my wife about it," he told me. "What I'm doing is a form of deception. It makes me feel guilty. It's almost as if I had a mistress. I'd feel guilty about that, and this is much the same. Every time I come close to telling her, something holds me back. I don't know what to do."

The strange thing is that he, of all people, should be able to ask his guides for advice on the situation. He is not prepared to do this because he is worried about what they might say about his marriage. Obviously, when one partner is keeping a secret from the other, there are deeper problems than this in the relationship, and he is not prepared to face them. Until he does, though, his personal and spiritual progress is held back. I am sure that once he gets this problem resolved he will become a much better medium than he is right now.

Saying Yes

Once you become a medium you will find that people will seek you out. It is amazing how quickly the word spreads, and you will soon find yourself with a group of supportive people who are on the same wavelength as you.

You may also find that some friends will leave your life. This is sad, of course, but if they are not developing at the same rate as you it is better to let them go. It is much more painful if you try to hang on and delay the inevitable. Be kind and gentle with your friends who doubt your mediumistic talents. If you were them, you would be acting in exactly the same way that they do.

Ignore the demands of skeptical people who insist that you "prove" your abilities. You will not convince these people no matter what you do. The fact that you know you can do these things is all that matters. It makes no difference at all what other people think.

You will also attract thc pcople who need your help. One medium I know feels that she is a magnet and subconsciously attracts needy people to her. "Once I was sitting on the beach enjoying the sun. Between me and the water was a family group of seven or eight people. They were having a great time, laughing and playing. I had my eyes closed and was almost asleep when I felt a shadow over me. I opened my eyes and one of the group was smiling down on me. He was in his late teens, I would think.

"The rest of his group were still playing in the sun, but this boy had a sadness in his eyes. We talked for a few minutes and then I gave him a message. He listened intently, wiped some tears from his eyes, thanked me and went back to his family. What made him come to me out of all the people on the beach that day? That sort of thing happens all the time. That's why my husband calls me a magnet!"

I have noticed that many mediums seem to have a special serenity and radiance about them, and it might be this that draws people to them.

You might decide to use your mediumistic gifts to help people who are close to you, rather than choose to work for the public. Either way, you will be able to help others. You will also experience the satisfactions and rewards that come from doing something really worthwhile.

19

Working in Pairs

Some people prefer to develop spiritually on their own. Others need more people contact and do it in groups. Still others prefer to do it in pairs.

There are many advantages to developing with someone else. Ego problems are unlikely, as you have probably been friends for many years. You will meet in each other's homes, where it is easy to relax. You are likely to have other interests in common besides the desire to make contact with your spirit guides. Thus, meetings are bound to cover a wide range of subjects, which makes them more enjoyable for both of you.

You will be able to support and encourage each other. This is important, as at times one person will develop more quickly than the other, and the person who is moving ahead will have to keep the other one motivated and interested. Finally, and possibly most importantly, your spirit guide may well speak to you through your friend.

Your friend might discover that she is a natural medium and be taken over temporarily by your spirit guide. This can be alarming the first few times it happens, but it will be made much easier with you there to offer support and help.

In fact, you should take turns relaxing and meditating and see if anything does come through. The messages should be recorded in some way, either on tape or written down. They then become a permanent record that can be referred to later.

I know many people who have successfully developed in pairs. Linda and Joy are two who immediately come to mind. They had been friends for more than forty years and had worked together to develop spiritually for most of that time. They began as teenagers playing with a ouija board, but quickly progressed beyond that stage.

"Joy suddenly started talking in a strange voice," Linda recalled. "I thought she was joking at first, but then I realized that she had an important message for me. Everything developed from that."

"We were just kids having fun," Joy recalled. "But even then, I think we both had a serious desire to know more."

These two, now in their late fifties, have an inner serenity that is obvious to everyone who meets them. They used to conduct psychic development classes behind a new age bookstore they owned. At one time they ran their own spiritualist church. Now they occasionally conduct workshops and seminars, but mainly offer advice and help to anyone who asks for it.

"It's a waste of time giving advice when it's not asked for," Joy told me. "It's never appreciated and seldom acted upon." However, if you ask them for advice, they will freely give it. It is hard to tell where the advice comes from: Linda, Joy, or their guides.

"Sometimes the answers surprise us," Linda said. "I can start to say something and then Joy will finish it off. Afterwards we don't know if we said it, or if it came through our guides. The only thing we do know is that most of the time the advice is good."

Linda and Joy are good examples of how close two people can become when they are both engaged in developing spiritually. They also work well on their own, but feel they do a better job when they are together.

"Just last week we helped a woman come to terms with her husband's death," Linda said. "He had died tragically, far too young, and his wife wouldn't let him go. It is good to mourn and be sad, but you shouldn't spend the rest of your life in that state. She had been grieving for more than a year, and came to see us dressed in black. It was so sad. While she was here, we could see her husband sitting at the dining table. He was wearing a suit with the tie undone. She said that is how he always looked when he came home from work."

"We got this strong feeling from him," Joy said, smoothly taking over from Linda. "He wanted his wife to let him go, so that he could move on. It grieved him to see his wife mourning for so long. He wanted her to let go and start her life again."

"We explained all this to the woman," Linda said. "Even while she was with us, we could see her start to change and look a little brighter. She called us a few days later to thank us, and she is now beginning to get on with her life."

"And her husband is able to move forward again, too."

"You see," Linda said, "we did that session together. Each of us could have done it on our own, but it was easier, smoother, and more effective to do it together." She smiled at Joy. "It's also more fun."

Linda and Joy are both widowed and are planning to set up a new spiritual center at a beach resort. "The climate's good all year round," Joy explained. "Also, we think we'll be able to do a lot of good there."

Linda and Joy exemplify the way two like-minded people can develop further together than they might have on their own. Their friendship has strengthened steadily over the years and they have developed the ability to read each other's mind. Perhaps you and a friend could develop in the same way.

Choose your friend carefully. Your first choice may not necessarily be the right one. Take your time. Be cautious, and ultimately you will be drawn to the right person. Do not rush things. You may start with informal get-togethers, perhaps over coffee or tea. You could lend each other books and discuss them afterwards.

When you feel ready, move on to experiments with the ouija board and pendulum. Practice progressive relaxations together. You might prepare a script and have one person read it while the other relaxes. You will be surprised at just how relaxed you can become when you feel confident, safe and secure with the other person.

Be supportive. Keep notes of your meetings. Practice sending telepathic messages to each other and record the results. Once you make contact with your guides your progress will be faster and more exciting. Until you do make contact, be patient. Linda and Joy have been working together for more than forty years and are still learning.

The wonderful thing about developing with a friend in this way is that you can still enjoy each other's company when the results are disappointing. Simply take your time, have fun, and you will be amazed at how far the two of you will progress.

20

The Past Life Connection

In my work as a hypnotherapist I have helped hundreds of people to recall their previous lives. For some years it was the specialty of my practice, as few other hypnotherapists were prepared to do it at the time. This interest ultimately led to invitations to speak at hypnotherapy conventions around the world. Eventually I wrote a book on the subject in the hope that it would encourage more hypnotherapists to explore this fascinating field.[1] Consequently, I have been involved with past life regressions for a long time. All the same, it was an accident that led me to discover the relationship between spirit guides and past life experiences.

Emily was a client who came to me for weight loss. She had previously attended a lecture I gave on reincarnation and came to me because of that. However, she did not want a past life regression as the idea scared her.

Until the age of fourteen Emily had been thin. She gained weight rapidly through her teenage years and had tried every diet that was available. Hypnosis was very much a last resort for her. She was well over 250 pounds and still gaining weight when she came to me.

As usual, I began the first session with a questionnaire concerning eating habits. Emily had a constant craving for chocolate, which was accentuated when she was under stress. She did very little exercising and preferred sodas to water. All of these things can be remedied with hypnosis.

For the first session I followed my standard weight loss procedure and made an appointment for her to see me again the following week. On this second visit I regressed her back to her fourteenth birthday in an attempt to find out what had happened at that time to cause the weight gain to start.

Emily was a good subject and regressed very easily. She remembered that her parents put on a family party to celebrate her birthday. Before dinner one of her cousins commented on her budding breasts and assaulted her through her clothes. Emily shut herself in her bedroom, but came out again before dinner. None of the adults appeared to notice the incident and her cousin apologized.

During the meal Emily looked across the table and found that her uncle was leering at her. She protectively crossed her arms and her uncle laughed. "You'll find many men looking at you," he said, "an attractive girl like you." Emily blushed and lowered her head.

These two incidents on the same evening were the underlying cause of her weight problem. Consciously, she had been able to remove the memories from her mind, but her subconscious, inner mind decided to make her unattractive to men. It did this by making her fat.

Emily was surprised that she had recalled these incidents and commented on how strange and unclean they had made her feel at the time. I explained that now, some twenty years later, those incidents were no longer of any account and that she could let them go. She agreed with this and immediately began to lose weight.

On the fourth session, Emily spontaneously regressed to a past life. This is something that happens occasionally, but I had not expected it to occur with Emily, as she was adamant that she did not want to experience any past lives.

In this past life Emily was a crude, coarse man in fifteenth-century England. (It is common for people to change sex in successive lifetimes. It means that we can experience lives as both sexes as we progress through different incarnations.) Emily was a landowner who brutalized his staff and terrified his children. However, he was tender and gentle with his wife, whom he adored. He appeared to have no friends, but drank heavily in a local pub with a group of like-minded acquaintances.

One night, returning home after a drinking session, he came across a peasant woman giving birth to a baby by the side of the road. His first thought, in his drunken state, was to shout a few obscenities and keep on walking. However, a memory of his wife almost dying while giving birth made him stop to see if he could help. He was bending over the woman, talking to her, when someone hit him over the head and he died.

It was a dramatic story, and an emotional one. Normally, while doing past life regressions, I tell subjects that they will see everything with a sense of detachment. This is so they will not feel the pain, grief, and sorrow that can otherwise occur during a regression. However, because I was not expecting Emily to regress to a past life, I had not done this and expected Emily to be highly emotional when she returned to full conscious awareness.

However, she came back to full consciousness in the usual way and was absolutely ecstatic. "That's the most amazing thing I've ever experienced!" she said.

"It will get even more amazing," I told her. "Now that you've unlocked the memories of that past life, you'll receive more and more insights over the next few days."

"She's my spirit guide!"

"Who?"

"My wife in that lifetime! She's my guide in this life!"

This was the first time I had experienced anything like this. "Are you sure?"

Emily laughed. "Of course! I saw her as clearly as I see you. No wonder she looks after me so well!"

Emily came back to see me again a week later. The excess weight was coming off steadily, and she was happy because a couple of people had mentioned how good she looked during the week. She was also anxious to tell me more about her regression.

"I was not that bad a man in that life," she said. "The times were hard and you had to be tough to survive. If I'd been soft on my workers, they'd have taken advantage. Anyway, I was soft on my family. That's where my greatest happiness was—just being at home surrounded by family."

This was a different version of the story from the one Emily had told so vividly under hypnosis. I gently pointed this out to her. She nodded.

"That's true. I had a reputation in the community of being wild and vicious. It was true in part, particularly when I was young, but I mellowed with age. My family loved me dearly. In fact, my wife never really got over my death. She took solace from the fact that I died trying to help someone else. Maybe that's why she looks after me so well in this lifetime!"

Since this experience many years ago I have met many other people who have also recognized their spirit guides while recalling their past lives. Spirit guides frequently are deceased relatives, so it should not have been a surprise to me when Emily spontaneously regressed and found her spirit guide. Certainly, the people I have spoken to who have seen their spirit guides in regressions have all taken it for granted.

I have not been able to discuss this phenomenon with all of my past life regression clients. Many have no interest in spirit guides, of course, and others may have felt embarrassed talking about it.

However, it has always been an extremely positive experience for the clients who do see their guides. For instance, I expected Emily to be upset with her violent death and rough life. In fact, she took that entirely for granted because she was totally focused on her discovery that her spirit guide in this lifetime was her wife in a past life. The positiveness of this far outweighed any of the incidents that most people would have found emotionally difficult.

Another interesting aspect is that many people who have not previously been able to see their spirit guides recognize them during a regression. It is very comforting for these people finally to discover what their guides look like.

The easiest way to have a past life regression is to go to a qualified hypnotherapist. Call several before deciding which one to go to. You want to feel relaxed and comfortable with the person you choose. You also want someone who is interested in past life regressions and does them frequently. Make sure that the hypnotherapist does not lead you to a particular past life in a period that he or she is interested in. You want your first past life regression to be completely random. The fact that you want to see your spirit guide means that your subconscious mind will automatically lead you to a specific past life. You do not want this to be overruled by the demands of the hypnotherapist.

Ask for a recording of the session. You will remember most of it anyway, but I've found that listening to a tape afterwards can sometimes help to unlock memories of the past life.

You may prefer to conduct your own past life regression. You will find this easy to do if you have practiced the progressive relaxation exercises in the previous chapters.

As usual, sit down in a quiet spot where you will not be disturbed. Make sure that you are warm and comfortable. Use some gentle, soothing relaxation music if you find it helpful.

Relax every part of your body as much as you can. When you feel totally limp, loose, and relaxed, picture a staircase in your mind. I picture a beautiful, curving staircase with a gleaming banister and a luxurious carpet. I sink into the thick pile of this carpet with every step. Your staircase might be completely different.

Double your relaxation with every step you take down this staircase. When you reach the bottom, pause and mentally check your body to make sure that every part is totally relaxed. Look around at the beautiful room you find yourself within. The furniture is luxurious and there are beautiful paintings on the walls. The sun is shining in through an open window and you can hear birds singing tunefully outside.

To your right is a long hallway. On each side is a row of closed doors. Behind each door is one of your many past lives. Slowly walk down the hallway, pausing outside each door until you find one that appears to invite you in. Reach out and open the door. Step inside, and instantly you'll find yourself at an important time in the particular past life that you are about to experience.

When you have had enough of that particular episode, mentally close your eyes and count to three. When you open them again you will have moved backwards or forwards through time to another situation in this lifetime. You can do this as many times as you wish.

Sometimes I simply close my eyes and count to three and see what situation confronts me. At other times, I close my eyes and ask to be placed in a situation which will help me understand this past life more clearly. For instance, I may want to see what I do for a living, what my partner looks like, what hobbies or interests I had, and so on.

Finally, I will ask to be taken to the very last day I spent in that particular incarnation. I will take myself through the moment of death, so that I am in spirit immediately after dying. That way, I can look down on myself and see what I looked like. I might even ask to attend my funeral and see the headstone on my grave. This can be useful if you are not sure of the time period you were living in. Many people in past centuries never went more than a few miles from their homes in any direction, so they often had no idea of the time period or even the country they lived in.

You may find that you recognize your spirit guide the very first time you regress back to a past life. Many people do. On the other hand, it might take several regressions before you recognize him or her. Be patient. There might be a particular reason your guides do not want to be seen.

You must respect that. They will become visible when the time is right.

Apart from the opportunity of seeing your spirit guides, you will find past life regressions helpful in many ways. Certain people will appear in many different lifetimes. The sexes and relationships will change, but you will recognize them all the same. You may find that even though each life is completely different, you were a certain type of person each time. For instance, you might have been a teacher in every life.

Perhaps you are a practical person in this lifetime. Your hands seem to be able to think for themselves. If this is the case, you may find that you were also good with your hands in every previous life.

Of course, the opposite might apply as well. You might be a plumber or builder this time, but discover that you were a philosopher last time. That means that you are exploring a new dimension of your being in this lifetime.

Past life regressions are fascinating. I love doing them because they are always helpful for my clients. Frequently, they provide an explanation for difficulties or problems the person is having in this lifetime. They can explain difficult relationships. And, of course, they can also bring you face to face with your spirit guide.

21

Other Invisible Helpers

Millions of spiritual creatures walk the earth unseen, both when we wake and when we sleep…

—John Milton, *Paradise Lost*, IV

As you become more and more conscious of your spirit guides and angel guardians you will also gradually become attuned to the nature spirits—sprites, elves, fairies and devas—who live everywhere, but are usually invisible. We humans have our guardian angels to look after us, but every living thing also has its own spirit to attend to its needs.

The angelic kingdom seems to be grouped into four main categories: the angels who work with humans;

angels working with animals; angels who work with the elements, and those who work with plant life.

Flower A. Newhouse, the gifted mystic and clairvoyant, saw nature spirits from an early age. Her first sighting was at the age of six when she was on the Staten Island Ferry and saw a group of tiny water sprites. She exclaimed to her friend: "Oh, look at the beautiful fairies!" Her friend could not see them, and thought Flower was simply playing a game. She responded by pointing out a variety of make-believe creatures. Flower was puzzled, as she could see the water sprites but saw none of the animals her friend described. She suddenly realized that her friend was making it all up. Flower was seeing a world that was invisible to most, and sadly, she came to the conclusion that she would never be able to talk about it with others.[1]

Flower was fortunate in being encouraged by three teachers in high school to talk about what she could see and angels became her life work. Ultimately, she wrote a series of wonderful books about angels.

It is a relatively common experience for people to glimpse these spirits, perhaps when gazing entranced at a waterfall or strolling through the woods. However, most people dismiss the experience as being simply a trick of the light or their imagination. Other people see these spirits and simply refuse to accept what they have seen.

Naturally, there are also a large number of people who do see nature spirits and allow them to help. Nature spirits love assisting people, especially when it is appreciated.

Years ago, I had a striking example of this. I was enjoying a pint of beer in a pub in Cornwall when a stranger came up to me and said:

"You look psychic. Tell me, do you have the gift?"

I was surprised at this greeting and tentatively replied that I was interested in the subject, and that he must also be psychic to have known that.

The man laughed at this reply and sat down. He was in his middle sixties, immaculately dressed in a tweed suit, and spoke with a strong West Country accent.

For half an hour he kept me enthralled as he told me about the fairies and elves he regularly saw on his farm. He called them his "elementals." With great enthusiasm, he told me how he looked after them and kept them happy, because he believed that without their help his farm would not be nearly as successful.

I accidentally broke the spell by asking him if he would like another drink. He looked around the room furtively, touched me on the shoulder, and asked me not to breathe a word of what he'd said to anyone in the room. He tapped the side of his nose.

"You and I—we know. But they don't. You're the first person I've ever talked to about this. It's our secret."

After he left I wondered why he had chosen me to speak to. He obviously had a great need to talk to someone about the invisible helpers on his farm, and I probably helped him enormously by simply listening to what he had to say.

There must be countless people like this Cornish farmer, who see nature spirits but have learned not to talk about them to others. It is sad to think that today, when people are able to freely discuss subjects that would have been taboo just a few years ago, we still cannot talk openly about spirit guides and nature spirits.

You are much more likely to see nature spirits if you approach nature with a degree of reverence. Close to my home is a successful flower shop owned by two women in their thirties. They both love their work, and their business has grown partly because of their talents at flower arranging, but especially because they both have excellent people skills. All of their customers become repeat customers and often end up becoming friends.

However, although they are both good at their work, one handles the flowers with great reverence and respect, while the other treats them more roughly. One day I commented on this, and the partner who treats the flowers with reverence replied, "I love all of nature and its mysteries. That's why I always ask my devas for permission to cut flowers, and then I have a duty to look after them as much as possible."

She told me this in a very casual, matter-of-fact way. I then asked her if her customers believed in nature spirits. "Some do and some don't. I can always tell, though. The ones who do get a special look in their eyes when they look at my flowers."

Those customers are obviously the ones who approach nature reverently. Along with respect, you need to be patient, positive, and open. When the time is right, the invisible helpers will make themselves known to you.

A friend of mine first saw water sprites on his honeymoon. He and his wife were enjoying a picnic lunch beside a majestic waterfall on a beautiful day. Although it was a popular tourist spot, they had timed it well and had the magnificent falls to themselves.

My friend, deeply in love and happier than he had ever been before, was relaxed and totally immersed in the beauty that surrounded him. Suddenly, he noticed a tiny person standing on a rock behind the falls. The person was almost transparent and my friend blinked several times, thinking it must be an illusion. He turned to his wife, but she had fallen asleep and he did not want to disturb her. He turned back to the figure, who was now waving to him. My friend waved back, and instantly saw hundreds of water sprites dancing and playing in the sparkling waters below the falls.

"It was the most beautiful experience of my whole life," he recalled. "It felt as if scales had dropped from my eyes and I was suddenly aware. I couldn't believe that I had lived for thirty years and not seen what was all around me." My friend was relaxed, happy, and enjoying nature when he first saw these water sprites. It was the ideal situation. If he had been stressed, rushed, or angry, the sprites would have remained unseen.

Nature has incredible healing qualities. If we allow it to, it can heal not just our bodies, but our hearts, minds and spirits as well. Green has always been considered a healing color and spending time with nature allows the different greens to restore and revitalize our physical. mental, emotional, and spiritual bodies again.

The nature spirits are well aware of this, and people who are relaxing in a natural environment and benefiting from this healing energy are also likely to be visited by them.

Nature spirits can be divided into four categories: the spirits of earth, air, fire, and water. There are different types of elementals relating to each category and, as mentioned before, there is also an archangel to watch over them.

Elves, gnomes, and tree devas belong to the earth element and are ruled by Uriel.

Undines, sea nymphs, naiads, and water sprites belong to the water element and are ruled by Gabriel.

Builders, zephyrs, sylphs, and air devas belong to the air element and are ruled by Raphael.

Salamanders and flamin belong to the fire element and are ruled by Michael.

People usually become attuned to seeing the elementals of one element, such as earth, before starting to notice them in the other areas. For instance, a lady I know sees elementals in trees, bushes and other small plants. However, she has yet to see any in or around the beautiful stream that passes by her property. Her husband can see the water sprites around the stream, but is not yet able to see the plant devas that his wife does. However, neither is concerned, as they know that when the time is right, they will be able to see all of the invisible helpers.

Many people never see the elves and spirits, but are simply aware of them. Miss Eva Longbottom told Sir Arthur Conan Doyle: "I have seen many fairies with my mind's eyes."[2] In other words, she believed the fairies were there, and although she could not see them with her normal eyes, she saw them easily when she used her "mind's eyes." One woman I know described her experiences with fairies in this way:

"When I'm out of doors, especially when I'm gardening or walking in the hills near my home, I sometimes feel a light brush, like a caress, on my arms or cheeks. It's somehow comforting, as it tells me that they're there. Of course, deep down I know they're there all the time, but it's nice to feel their presence as well."

She explained that the touch was so gentle that it was almost imperceptible. "It's not like an insect landing on my arm. That's heavy in comparison. If I weren't attuned to it, I doubt if I'd even notice it."

This lady hopes one day to be able to see her invisible helpers, but is not concerned if it never happens. "If they want me to see them, they'll allow it," she says.

Robert Bray, a geologist and mystic, has seen nature spirits in many rock formations. He believes that they nurture and encourage the growth and psychic potential of crystals. "It's not something I'd discuss with everyone," he admits, "but when I'm out in the field and see them, I know that we're close to something that's geologically important. Being able to see them gives me a hidden edge that my colleagues don't have. However, it also gives me more responsibility. In my job we're digging up rocks and minerals all the time. I need to make sure that we do this in a way that does least damage to the environment."

Nature spirits can be found all over the globe, even at both poles. With their help we can achieve miracles.

A startling example is the Findhorn Community's famous garden on a windswept part of northern Scotland. The soil is sandy and full of stones. By rights, only plants used to this inhospitable climate should be able to survive, but the members of the community successfully grow a wide range of vegetables, fruits, flowers, and trees there.

They have succeeded because they asked for and followed the advice of the nature spirits. Dorothy Maclean, a gifted mystic and clairvoyant, started the project by contacting the spirit of a garden pea. From this modest beginning she began communicating with all the devas in the garden. Dorothy has never seen a nature spirit, though she sometimes receives an "impression of a pattern, a shape or a color."[3] However, she hears them clairaudiently.

Dorothy began after being told: "Be open and seek into the glorious realms of Nature with sympathy and understanding."[4] This is exactly what you need to do to make contact with this invisible world. Dorothy Maclean originally felt nervous, afraid and incapable, but fortunately Peter Caddy, one of the other founders of Findhorn, had no such qualms and said, "Nonsense, of course you can (do it)."[5] And, indeed, she could. Every day she received practical information about the garden, and the results are seen every day by the numerous visitors the community attracts.

At one time the county horticultural adviser came to examine the soil. He said it was lacking certain nutrients, but on testing it found the soil was perfectly balanced. The project was still in its establishment phase at this time, in the middle 1960s, and the Findhorn founders did not feel able to tell him about their invisible helpers.[6]

I believe that every keen gardener has contact with these invisible helpers, whether realizing it or not. They may experience a gut feeling to plant something in a certain position, and not question where the feeling or intuition came from. My father-in-law has the most incredible collection of orchids that I have ever seen. He has no interest in psychic matters whatsoever, but his success with orchids is largely due to the fact that he acts on his hunches and feelings.

A married couple I know have had an interesting experience with the devas. The wife, who had never gardened before, decided that she needed as much help as possible, and summoned the invisible helpers to her aid. Her husband, an experienced gardener, scoffed at this idea. They now have a magnificent flower garden, cared for by the wife and her invisible helpers, and an indifferent vegetable garden, tended by the husband. He cannot understand how his wife can be so successful at something she knows little about. He still laughs when his wife talks about her invisible helpers, but is starting to become more aware. I am sure that when he does, his vegetable garden will flourish beyond all his expectations.

The devas asked for a wild area to be left in the Findhorn garden where the nature spirits would be undisturbed. If you do this in your own garden, you will find the nature spirits rewarding you in other ways. You may find a plant that was always sickly will regain its health. Perhaps you will receive a more bountiful crop than usual from a certain plant. Maybe your vegetables will taste sweeter. The rewards may come in hidden ways, but they will certainly be there. We have had a wild area in our garden for at least twenty years, and even our cat stays away from it. We all find it a restful, tranquil spot and enjoy meditating close by.

22

Conclusion

We have covered a great deal of ground in these pages. By now you will know how to make the best use of your guardian angels and spirit guides. It can be very comforting to know that we have protection, advice and guidance whenever we need it, simply by asking our guardian angels or spirit guides for help.

Now it is up to you. Spiritual growth will fill your life with happiness, love, joy, and complete fulfillment. Allow your angels and guides to help you live a life of success, abundance, and continual growth.

Please don't simply read this book and then put it away. That is what most people do when exposed to something new. There is a famous Chinese proverb that says: "I dreamed a thousand new paths…I woke and walked the old one." Please don't do that. Dream of the new paths, and then follow the one that seems right for you.

Use this book as a workbook. Work through the different exercises. Keep a record of your results and findings. We all progress in stages. Sometimes we move ahead quickly, while at other times we feel as if we are simply marking time. By keeping records you can look back and see how far you have actually progressed. This can be very reassuring during the slower periods.

Be patient. You will not master everything in this book overnight. Nothing worthwhile happens without effort. Remain positive and confident, and the results will come, probably more quickly than you think.

You may find that you would rather work with your guardian angel than with your spirit guides, or vice versa. That is fine. We are all different and what appeals to you may not necessarily appeal to someone else. In practice, you will probably find that you use your guardian angels for some things and your spirit guides for others.

Remember that the underlying spiritual message is exactly the same whether you choose to work with guardian angels, spirit guides, nature spirits, animals or anything else that interests you. All of them serve as symbolic representations of the love, help, and guidance that is available to you from the universe. They want you to use them to help your progress and development as you make your way through this incarnation.

You can do much of this on your own, but your progress will be faster and more enjoyable if you develop with a like-minded person. If you have no one in mind at the moment, ask your guardian angel to bring that person to you. You will both benefit by meeting each other.

It is fine if you still prefer to do it on your own. We are all different and there is no right or wrong way of developing. Some people need the camaraderie and support of a group, others want just one or two other people to help them, and others prefer to work on their own. You may even start on your own and gradually find yourself drawn into a group. The universe works in mysterious ways and will ensure that you meet the right people for your growth and development when it feels that you are ready.

I hope you have enjoyed this book. If it helps you make contact with your guardian angel and spirit guides, I will be very happy.

Notes

Chapter 1

1. Martin Luther, *Table Talk*, trans. William Hazlitt (1821; reprint, London: HarperCollins, 1995), 273. This book of Martin Luther's sayings was published posthumously in 1566 and contains many of Luther's quotes, epigrams, and advice given over the dinner table.

2. Paola Giovetti, *Angels: the Role of Celestial Guardians and Beings of Light* (York Beach: Samuel Weiser Inc., 1993), 4.

3. Keith Crim, Roger A. Bullard, and Larry D. Shinn, eds. *The Perennial Dictionary of World Religions* (San Francisco: Harper and Row, 1989), 36. Originally published as *Abingdon*

Dictionary of World Religions by Abingdon Press, Nashville, 1981.

4. The Holy Bible, Col. 2:18. The varying attitude of the Christian Church toward angels began with St. Paul's condemnation. However, at the Council of Nicea in 325 A.D., a belief in angels became part of Church doctrine. A few years later, in 343 A.D., the Synod of Laodicaea declared worship of angels to be idolatry. Four hundred years after this the seventh Ecumenical Synod introduced a limited number of archangels. All quotes from the Bible in this book are from the King James Version of 1611, known in Britain as the Authorized Version.

5. The word *angel* appears 292 times in the Bible, but there are many other places where angels are referred to as cherubim, seraphs, thrones, powers, ministering spirits, etc. The major references to angels in the Bible are: Gen. 3:23–24; Gen. 16:7–13; Gen. 22:10–12; Gen. 28:12; Gen. 32:25; Exod. 3:2; Deut. 33:2; Judg. 13:2–5; Judg. 13:20; 1 Kings 19:4–8; Job 38:7; Psalms 68:17; Psalms 91:11–12; Psalms 103:20; Isa. 6:1–7; Dan. 3:24–28; Dan. 6:22; Dan. 8:15–17; Dan. 10:5–6; Dan. 10:12–14; Tob. 5:4; Matt. 1:19–24; Matt. 2:19–20; Matt. 13:41–42; Matt. 16:27; Matt. 18:10; Matt. 22:30; Matt. 28:2–6; Luke 1:11–12; Luke 1:26; Luke 2:8; Luke 2:21; Luke 16:22; Luke 24:2–4; John 20:12; Acts 1:10–11; Acts 12:6–9; Acts 8:26;

Acts 12:23; Acts 27:23–24; Cor. 13:1; Heb. 1:14; Rev. 22:8.

6. Linda Georgian, *Your Guardian Angels* (New York: Simon and Schuster, 1994), 39.

7. The Hindus have an entire cosmology of angels. Gandharvas are the angels of music; Yakshas and Kinnaras are semi-divine angels, though the Yakshas are more highly evolved; Apsarases are female angels who are adept at dancing and music; and sthana-devatas are presiding deities. There are five types of sthana-devatas: a grama-devata looks after and protects a village; the vana-devata protects the woods; a griha-devata protects a house; a nagar-devata protects a town; and a kshetra-pala protects fields and farms.

8. The Bhagavad Gita, III, ii:12.

9. Joan of Arc, quoted in *Do You Have a Guardian Angel?* by John Ronner (Murfreesboro: Mamre Press, 1985), 108.

10. Encyclopedia Britannica, *Macropaedia*, vol. 1, x875. (Chicago: Encyclopedia Britannica, Inc., 15th ed., 1974).

11. Brian Inglis with Ruth West and the Koestler Foundation, *The Unknown Guest* (London: Chatto and Windus Limited, 1987), 9.

12. C. G. Jung, *Memories, Dreams, Reflections* (London: Collins and Routledge & Kegan Paul, 1963), 302.

13. Hope Price, *Angels: True Stories of How They Touch Our Lives* (London: Macmillan London, 1993), 5.

14. *This England*, Cheltenham, Winter 1982. First-person account by Captain Cecil Wightwick Hayward. There are numerous stories of angel visitations during World War I. Some people claim it all began when a short story called "The Bowmen" was published in the *London Evening News* on September 29, 1914. This story contains a description of a long line of Agincourt archers who kill ten thousand Germans, none of whom show any signs of injuries. After this story appeared many people came forward who claimed to have seen angels in the battlefields. These accounts have been called "tragic self-deception" by Melvin Harris in his skeptical book *Investigating the Unexplained* (Buffalo: Prometheus Press, 1986).

15. G. Don Gilmore, "The Nature of Angel Forms," article in *Angels and Mortals*, comp. Maria Parisen (Wheaton: Quest Books, 1990), 7.

16. However, it can still be done, as the example of the Angels of Mons shows. A more intriguing example can be found in *Conjuring Up Philip* by I. M. Owen and M. Sparrow (New York: Pocket

Books, 1977). This book tells how several parapsychologists in Toronto created a "ghost" by inventing his personality. They then vividly believed that he was real and discovered that because of this, he actually became real. Although he never appeared to them, he did create sounds, answer questions, and levitate objects. Some of these experiments were done on television, enabling thousands of people to witness them.

17. Pseudo-Dionysius the Areopagite, *The Mystical Theology and the Celestial Hierarchies* (Godalming: The Shrine of Wisdom, 1949). Pseudo-Dionysius was probably an Armenian monk whose writings were highly commended by a number of the early popes. His main works are: *Celestial Hierarchies*; *On the Ecclesiastical Hierarchy*; *Ten Letters*, and *The Divine Names*. He is referred to as "Pseudo" Dionysius because the early Christians thought he was the famous Greek judge of the same name who is mentioned in the Bible. It was not until the Middle Ages that scholars realized that Pseudo-Dionysius had written his works in the sixth century and could not possibly be the same Dionysius who is in the Bible. Consequently, he is now known as Pseudo-Dionysius, or, less kindly, False-Dionysius.

18. There are at least thirteen other classifications of the celestial hierarchy, which all vary slightly from this list compiled by Pseudo-Dionysius. For

instance, in his book *The Magus*, Francis Barrett changes the positions of the Powers and Virtues and adds three more to the list: Innocents, Martyrs, and Confessors. (Francis Barrett, *The Magus*, Book 2, 1801, 34–45.) Most of the other arrangements are listed in *A Dictionary of Angels* by Gustav Davidson (New York: The Free Press), 336–337.

19. Silver RavenWolf, *Angels: Companions in Magic* (St. Paul: Llewellyn Publications, 1996), 41.

20. Emanuel Swedenborg wrote many books, available from the Swedenborg Foundation, 139 East 23rd St., New York, NY 10010. Arguably, his most approachable work is *Heaven and Hell*, originally published in 1758. The Foundation published an excellent translation of this book by George F. Dole in 1976.

21. James H. Hindes, "The Hierarchies," article in *Angels and Mortals*, comp. Maria Parisen, 118–119.

22. The text of this prayer is: "Hail Mary, full of grace, the Lord is with you. Blessed are you among women and blessed is the fruit of your womb, Jesus. Holy Mary, Mother of God, pray for us sinners, now and at the hour of our death. Amen."

23. Linda Georgian, *Your Guardian Angels*, 53.

24. Sean Kelly and Rosemary Rogers, *Saints Preserve Us!* (New York: Random House, 1993).

25. Te Ua Haumene, quoted in *Like Them That Dream: The Maori and the Old Testament* by Bronwyn Elsmore (Tauranga: The Tauranga Moana Press, 1985), 109.

26. Ruzbehan Baqli, quoted in *Angels: Messengers of the Gods* by Peter Lamborn Wilson (London: Thames and Hudson, 1980), 41.

27. Silver RavenWolf, *Angels: Companions in Magic*, 47–48.

28. Encyclopedia Brittanica, *Micropaedia*, vol. 6, 15th ed., 1983, 352.

29. John Ronner, *Do You Have a Guardian Angel?* (Murfreesboro: Mamre Press, 1985), 19.

30. Encyclopedia Britannica, *Micropaedia*, vol. 4, 15th ed., 1983, 64.

31. John Milton, quoted in *England in Literature*, Robert C. Pooley, George K. Anderson, Paul Farmer and Helen Thornton, eds. (Chicago: Scott, Foresman and Company, 1963), 219.

32. Richard Webster, *Feng Shui for Beginners* (St. Paul: Llewellyn Publications, 1997), 6–7.

Chapter 2

1. Thomas Aquinas, quoted in *A Rustle of Angels* by Marilynn Carlson Webber and William D. Webber (Grand Rapids: Zondervan Publishing House, 1994), 25.

2. Harvey Humann, *The Many Faces of Angels* (Marina del Rey: DeVorss and Company, 1986), 4.

3. Father Alessio Parente, *Send Me Your Guardian Angels, Padre Pio* (Foggia: Editions, 1984), 113.

4. Harvey Humann, *The Many Faces of Angels*, 5–6.

5. Rosemary Ellen Guiley, *Angels of Mercy* (New York: Pocket Books, 1994), 59–60.

6. There are many books available today that talk about near-death experiences. I feel that the book that started the whole genre is still the best: *Life After Life* by Raymond A. Moody, Jr., M.D. (St. Simon's Island: Mockingbird Books, 1975). It is worth noting that people from other cultures do not necessarily have the same near-death experiences we have in the West. In India, for instance, researchers found that messengers took the people undergoing near-death experiences to the netherworld. These messengers are probably Yamdoots, the couriers of death. Here, a gatekeeper consulted a book or some papers, and told the person that the

messenger had made a mistake and brought the wrong person. After being told this, the messengers simply deposited the person back in his or her body. Elizabeth L. Hillstrom, *Testing the Spirits* (Downers Grove: InterVarsity Press, 1995), 91.

7. Southern Centre of Theosophy, Robe, Australia, comp. *Devas and Men* (Adyar: The Theosophical Publishing House, 1977), 70.

8. Paola Giovetti, *Angels: The Role of Celestial Guardians and Beings of Light*, 119.

9. Harvey Humann, *The Many Faces of Angels*, 12.

10. Peter King, "Who Was the Fourth Man?" article in *Fate* magazine, March 1967.

11. Harvey Humann, *The Many Faces of Angels*, 12.

12. Frank Smythe, *Adventures of a Mountaineer* (London: J. H. Dent and Company, 1940).

13. John Ronner, *Do You Have a Guardian Angel?* 106.

14. Migene González-Wippler, *The Complete Book of Spells, Ceremonies and Magic* (New York: Crown Publishers, Inc., 1978), 97. *Shekinah* is often related to archangel Metraton, and is believed to surround married couples while they are making love.

15. Brad Steiger, *ESP: Your Sixth Sense* (New York: Award Books, 1976), 34–35. William Cox wrote

up his results in the *Journal of the American Society for Psychical Research*, vol. 50, no. 3.

16. Richard Webster, *Omens, Oghams and Oracles* (St. Paul: Llewellyn Publications, 1995), 39–41. An oracle tree is a personal tree that relates well to you. You can find one by hugging trees that appeal to you. When you find one that responds in a particularly favorable manner to your hug, you will have your own personal oracle tree.

Chapter 3

1. Bruce A. Vance, *Dreamscape: Voyage in an Alternate Reality* (Wheaton: Quest Books, 1989).
2. C. G. Jung, *Memories, Dreams, Reflections*, 302.
3. Thomas Aquinas, quoted in *Gods, Spirits, Cosmic Guardians* by Hilary Evans (Wellingborough: The Aquarian Press, 1987), 45.
4. Gustav Davidson, *A Dictionary of Angels* (New York: Free Press, 1967), xii.
5. Dion Fortune, *Psychic Self-Defence* (Society of the Inner Light, 1930; reprint, New York: Samuel Weiser Inc., 1981), 76.

6. James T. Fields, "Fiction and its Eminent Authors" (lecture). This quote can be found in the *Encyclopedia of Psychic Science* by Nandor Fodor, 382.
7. Peter Lamborn Wilson, *Angels: Messengers of the Gods*, 73.
8. Joel Goldsmith, quoted in *The Many Faces of Angels* by Harvey Humann, 45.
9. Alexandra David-Neel, *Magic and Mystery in Tibet* (1932, reprint New York: University Books, 1965). Viking Penguin and Sphere Books have also reprinted this modern-day classic.

Chapter 4

1. Sophy Burnham, *A Book of Angels* (New York: Ballantine Books, 1990), 56.
2. Richard Webster, *Talisman Magic* (St. Paul: Llewellyn Publications, 1995), 63–64.
3. For further information on colors and numerology see *Aura Reading for Beginners* and *Chinese Numerology*, both by Richard Webster (St. Paul: Llewellyn Publications, 1998).

Chapter 5

1. "Charles W. Leadbeater," article in *The Theosophist*, vol. 63, no. 1, 453.

2. The Apocrypha. There are many translations available. The most accessible is the Nonesuch Press edition of 1924, reprinted in 1962 by University Books, Inc., New Hyde Park. The University of Chicago Press published "an American translation" by Edgar J. Goodspeed in 1938. Harper Publishers, New York, published a translation of The Book of Tobit by Frank Zimmerman in 1958.

3. Asmodeus is described as a "raging fiend" in The Book of Tobit, 3:8. The name Asmodeus is derived from the Persian word *ashma daeva*. However, the Jews also accepted him as an evil spirit. He is believed to have made Noah drunk, and to have invented music, dancing and dreams. Today he is in charge of all the gambling establishments in hell. (Gustav Davidson, *A Dictionary of Angels*, 57–58.)

4. John Ronner, *Do You Have a Guardian Angel?* 17.

5. Sandra L. Zimdars-Swartz, *Encountering Mary: From La Salette to Medjugorje* (Princeton, NJ: Princeton University Press, 1991), 50.

Chapter 7

1. Peter Lamborn Wilson, *Angels: Messengers of the Gods*, 71.
2. Encyclopaedia Britannica, *Macropaedia*, vol. 2, 1100.
3. William Blake, quoted in *The Many Faces of Angels* by Harvey Humann, 27.
4. Catherine Blake, quoted in *England in Literature*, Robert C. Pooley, ed. (Chicago: Scott, Foresman and Company, 1963), 338.
5. Malcolm Godwin, *Angels: An Endangered Species* (New York: Simon and Schuster, 1990), 6.
6. George Frideric Handel, quoted in *The Oxford Junior Companion to Music* by Percy A. Scholes (Oxford: Oxford University Press, 1954), 169.

Chapter 11

1. Julian Hawthorne, *Hawthorne and His Circle*. This quote from Nathaniel Hawthorne's son can be found in *Encyclopaedia of Psychic Science by Nandor Fodor* (1934, reprint New York: University Books, Inc., 1966), 154.

2. Xenophon, *Memorabilia Socratis*, A. R. Cluer, B.A., ed. Boston: Henry and Company, 1893, 124.
3. J. B. Greatbarr, ed. *The Saint Augustine Collection* (Newcastle: New Growth Centre, 1964), 212.
4. Eugene Burger, *Spirit Theater* (New York: Kaufman and Greenberg, 1986), 37.
5. David P. Abbott, *Behind the Scenes with the Mediums* (Chicago: The Open Court Publishing Company, 1907), 53–54.
6. George Templeton Strong, *The Diary of George Templeton Strong*, Allan Nevins and Milton H. Thomas, eds., vol. 2 (New York: Macmillan and Company, 1952), 244–245.
7. Paul Kurtz, "Spiritualists, Mediums and Psychics," article in *A Skeptic's Handbook of Parapsychology*, Paul Kurtz, ed. (Buffalo: Prometheus Press, 1985), 180.
8. Nat Freedland, *The Occult Explosion* (New York: Berkeley Publishing Company, 1972), 76–77. Nettie Maynard, one of the White House mediums, published her book *Was Abraham Lincoln a Spiritualist?* in 1891.
9. Alfred Russel Wallace, quoted in "A Critical Historical Overview of Parapsychology," article by Ray Hyman in *A Skeptic's Handbook of Parapsychology*, Paul Kurtz, ed. Hyman quotes from

The Psycho-Physiological Sciences and Their Assailants, A. R. Wallace, J. R. Buchanan, D. Lyman, E. Sargent, eds. (Boston: Colby and Rich, 1878).

10. Hélène Smith was the pseudonym of Catherine Elise Muller (1861–1929). Her life and work were documented and studied by Théodore Flournoy, the eminent Swiss psychologist, who became her friend and wrote extensively about her.

11. Terence Hines, *Pseudoscience and the Paranormal* (Buffalo: Prometheus Press, 1988), 25.

12. Théodore Flournoy, *Des Indes á la Planéte Mars* (Geneva: Atar, 1899), quoted in *Gods, Spirits, Cosmic Guardians* by Hilary Evans, 49.

13. Andrew Jackson Davis, *The Principles of Nature, Her Divine Revelations, and a Voice to Mankind*, 1847, 675–676.

14. Hereward Carrington, *The Physical Phenomena of Spiritualism* (Boston: Herbert B. Turner and Company, 1907), 372.

15. Viscount Adare, *Experiences in Spiritualism with Mr. D. D. Home*, quoted in *Spiritualists, Mediums and Psychics* by Paul Kurtz, 190.

16. *Proceedings of the SPR*, London, 1889, 6:98–127.

17. Sir William Crookes, "Notes of an Inquiry into the Phenomena called Spiritual during the Years

1870–73." *Quarterly Journal of Science*, January 1874, reprint in *A Voice from Beyond* by Gilbert Roller (New York: Popular Library, 1975), 63–92.

Chapter 12

1. Paul Beard, *Inner Eye, Listening Ear* (Tasburgh: Pilgrim Books, 1992), 4.
2. Jon Klimo, *Channeling* (Los Angeles: Jeremy P. Tarcher, Inc., 1987), 80. Some four thousand years ago the ancient Chinese used a planchette-like instrument. It was a branched bough, much like a divining rod, which was held by two people. The spirits were then asked to answer questions and the device would start moving, spelling out the message on paper or sand.
3. Jon Klimo, *Channeling*, 197.
4. David C. Knight, *The ESP Reader* (New York: Grosset and Dunlop, Inc., 1969), 257.
5. Ann Bridge, *Moments of Knowing* (London: Hodder and Stoughton Limited, 1970), 60–63.
6. Casper S. Yost, *Patience Worth: A Psychic Mystery* (London: Skeffington and Son Limited, 1916), 9–10. In this book (35–36), Yost further describes Pearl Curran: "There seems nothing abnormal

about her. She is an intelligent, conscientious woman, a member of the Episcopalian church, but not especially zealous in affairs of religion, a talented musician, a clever and witty conversationalist, and a charming hostess."

7. *New York Times* review, quoted in *ESP: Your Sixth Sense* by Brad Steiger, 144.

8. Patience Worth, quoted in *Patience Worth: A Psychic Mystery* by Casper S. Yost, 262.

9. William Stainton Moses, quoted in *Encyclopaedia of Psychic Science* by Nandor Fodor, 19.

10. Mrs. Howitt-Watts, *Pioneers of Spiritual Reformation*, 1883. This book was largely a biography of the author's father. William Howitt also wrote many books himself, fiction and nonfiction. His best-known work is *The History of the Supernatural in all Ages and Nations and in all Churches, Christian and Pagan, Demonstrating a Universal Faith.* This massive tome was published in two volumes in 1863.

11. Harvey Day, *Occult Illustrated Dictionary* (London: Kaye and Ward Limited, 1975), 16. The Rev. George Vale Owen's automatic writing was published as a series in the Weekly Dispatch. He was forced to leave the Church of England because of these articles and became a spiritualist pastor. He wrote many books, particularly *Life Beyond the Veil*

(five volumes). A year after his death Frederick H. Haines published his book A *Voice from Heaven*, created by automatic writing received from the spirit of the Rev. Owen.

12. Jeffrey Goodman, *Psychic Archaeology* (Berkeley: Berkeley Publishing and G. P. Putnam's, 1977), 3–8.

13. Susy Smith, *Widespread Psychic Wonders* (New York: Ace Publishing Corporation, 1970), 100.

14. Sir Oliver Lodge, *Raymond or Life and Death* (London, Methuen and Company, 1916) Also, Sir Oliver Lodge, *Raymond Revised* (London: Methuen and Company, 1922).

15. *Sir Oliver Lodge: Psychical Researcher and Scientist* (Rutherford: Farleigh Dickinson University Press, 1974), 202. The "Myers" referred to was Frederick Myers, a leading psychical investigator and friend of Sir Oliver Lodge. He died in 1901.

16. Jon Klimo, *Channeling*, 110–111.

17. C. H. Broad, preface, *Swan on a Black Sea* by Geraldine Cummins (London, Routledge and Kegan Paul, 1965), 7.

18. Ruth Montgomery, *The World Before* (New York: Coward, McCann and Geoghegan, Inc., 1976), xiii.

19. Brian Inglis with Ruth West and the Koestler Foundation, *The Unknown Guest*, 196–197.

20. Gambier Bolton, quoted in *Encyclopaedia of Psychic Science* by Nandor Fodor, 375.

21. More information on the pendulum is found in *Dowsing for Beginners* by Richard Webster (St. Paul: Llewellyn Publications, 1996). Chapter 7 of *How to Develop Your Psychic Power* by Richard Webster (London: Martin Breese Limited, 1988) contains psychic experiments that can be done with a pendulum.

22. Max Maven, *Max Maven's Book of Fortunetelling* (New York: Prentice Hall, 1992), 212.

23. Chelsea Quinn Yarbro, *Messages from Michael* (New York: Playboy Paperbacks, 1979) and Chelsea Quinn Yarbro, *More Messages from Michael* (New York: Berkley Books, 1986).

Chapter 17

1. Tudor Pole, quoted in *Inner Eye, Listening Ear* by Paul Beard, 106.

2. Dr. Dees, "In the Dark," article in *Seance* 3, Spring 1989 (Ellicott City: Seance), 13.

3. Jean Ritchie, *Inside the Supernatural* (London: Fontana Books, 1992), 122.

4. Jean Ritchie, *Inside the Supernatural*, 103–109.

Chapter 18

1. Doris Stokes and Linda Dearsley, *Voices in My Ear: The Autobiography of a Medium* (London: Futura Publications Limited, 1980), 85.

Chapter 19

1. Richard Webster, *Cashing In On Past Lives* (Auckland: Brookfield Press, 1989).

Chapter 21

1. Stephen Isaac, Ph.D., ed., *Flower A. Newhouse's Angels of Nature* (Wheaton: Quest Books, 1995), xiv.
2. Eva Longbottom, quoted in *The Coming of the Fairies* by Arthur Conan Doyle (1921, reprint, New York: Samuel Weiser, Inc., 1979), 168.
3. The Findhorn Community, *The Findhorn Garden* (London: Turnstone Books and Wildwood House, 1976), 59.
4. Dorothy Maclean, *To Hear the Angels Sing* (Issaquah: Lorian Press, 1980), 47.

5. Peter Caddy, quoted in *To Hear the Angels Sing* by Dorothy Maclean, 48.
6. Dorothy Maclean, *To Hear the Angels Sing*, 61–62.

Glossary

Angel. From the Greek word *angelos*, which in turn comes from the Hebrew *mal'akh*, which means "messenger." Consequently, an angel is a messenger from God. Angels are spiritual beings who attend to God.

Apport. An object that appears at seances. There seems to be no limit to the objects that can appear. They can include stones, crystals, jewelry, flowers, and items that have been lost previously by one of the attendees.

Automatic writing. The ability to write without conscious control, in other words, from a source outside oneself. This can include handwriting and typing. The writing is done without conscious muscular or mental effort.

Celestial Hierarchy. A listing of angels in their holy order. It was first written down by Pseudo-Dionysius the Areopagite in the sixth century. It consists of nine choirs of angels, grouped into three triads. The angels in the first triad are always in the presence of God and are known as "God's faithful angels." The angels in the second triad are the ministering and organizing angels. They are detached and universal in outlook, and only occasionally known to assist humans. The angels of the third triad are the ones most involved with what happens here on earth.

First Triad

1. Seraphim.
2. Cherubim.
3. Thrones.

Second Triad

4. Dominions.
5. Virtues.
6. Powers.

Third Triad

7. Principalities.
8. Archangels.
9. Angels.

Channeling. The ability to bring an intelligence through from a different level of reality for the purpose of promoting philosophical and spiritual beliefs.

Control. The main spirit that comes through to a medium. His or her control can then summon other spirits to the seance. The name *control* is used because the discarnate spirit takes control of the medium while he or she is in a trance.

Deva. From a Sanskrit word meaning "shining one," this is another word for nature spirits, but especially relates to wood spirits.

Discarnate. Meaning "without a body," this is the term used in seances to indicate people who have passed over to the other side.

Ectoplasm. A substance that some mediums claim to be able to produce. It is often produced from the mouth or nostrils and gradually forms into a human shape, often a face or limb rather than the full form. Ectoplasm is sensitive to light and can be produced only in the dark. The term *ectoplasm* was coined by Charles Richet (1850–1935), a Nobel Prize winner and leading psychic researcher.

Enoch. Author of the Book of Enoch, and the only human being who has ever been transformed into an angel. He is now known as Metatron, the "King of Angels," who is "Closest to the Throne." He has been described as between eight and thirteen feet tall, with thirty-six wings, and countless eyes to watch over the entire universe.

Fallen angels. Lucifer, the Light Bearer, was the most beautiful of God's angels. Unfortunately, he rebelled against God's authority and, along with many other angels who supported him, was thrown out of heaven into hell.

Guardian angel. A personal angel who watches over us and provides protection and guidance all the way through our lives. The guardian angel arrives at birth, stays with us during this lifetime, and escorts us to the other side when life is over.

Medium. A person who is able to act as the organ of communication, or mouthpiece, for departed spirits. Usually, the medium goes into a trance and is then taken over by the spirit for the duration of the message. The word *medium* means "go-between," which is the role that the medium takes during a seance.

Mediumship. The ability to bring spirits of the deceased through to communicate with the living.

Metatron. See **Enoch.**

Ouija board. A device used to make contact with the spirits of people who have died. It displays the letters of the alphabet and the numbers 0 to 9. An upturned glass or planchette is placed over the board and moves from letter to letter spelling out messages.

Planchette. The planchette is the pointer or indicator used with the ouija board. Originally it consisted of two small wheels, or castors, with a pen or pencil fixed in front. When fingers were placed on it lightly, the planchette would move and the pen would write messages. Today, the planchette usually has three small wheels, or felt pads that slide across the board.

Seance. A gathering of people who attempt to receive messages from the spirit world. A seance is generally conducted by a medium.

Sitting. This is the term used when someone has a session with a medium.

Spirit. The spirit of a deceased person. It also refers to that part of the person that survives physical death. In channeling, the spirit may never have been a human being.

Spirit guides. The souls of people who have passed over into the next life and assist the living. Spiritualist mediums often have guides who have been reincarnated many times and developed enormous wisdom. Consequently, they are frequently highly evolved souls, such as Native American chiefs, Chinese sages, Egyptian priests and other wise people from past ages. Your personal spirit guides are usually, but not always, deceased relatives. They are caring souls who have a desire to help people in this incarnation.

Spiritualism. A religion that believes in continuous life based on communication, by means of mediumship, with the inhabitants of the spirit world. Spiritualists believe that people's spirits survive death as discarnates, and that they can communicatc with thc living.

Table-tipping. A method of contacting the spirits that was very popular in Victorian times. Two or more people rested their fingers on top of a table and asked questions. The table would move, tapping one leg to answer questions. One tap of the table leg meant "yes," two taps meant "no," and three taps meant "maybe." Complete messages could be spelled out by using the letters of the alphabet. One tap would indicate "A," two taps "B," and so on.

Thought forms. Creations consisting of concentrated energy. When a thought is constructed using strong emotions, and sent out into the world, it can be a powerful force for good or ill.

Trance. An altered state of consciousness, commonly associated with hypnotism. In this state, conscious attention is taken away from the normal senses temporarily. Mediums are able to enter trance very quickly to allow their controls to take over temporarily.

Suggested Reading

Adler, Mortimer J. *The Angels and Us*. New York: Macmillan Publishing Co. Inc., 1982.

Anderson, Joan Wester. *Where Angels Walk*. Sea Cliff: Barton and Brett, 1992.

Andrews, Ted. *How to Meet and Work With Spirit Guides*. St. Paul: Llewellyn Publications, 1992.

Beard, Paul. *Inner Eye, Listening Ear*. Norwich: Pilgrim Books, 1992.

Belhayes, Iris and Enid. *Spirit Guides: We Are Not Alone*. San Diego: ACS Publications, 1986.

Bloom, William. *Devas, Fairies and Angels: A Modern Approach*. Glastonbury: Gothic Image Publications, 1986.

Brandon, R. *The Spiritualists*. New York: Alfred A. Knopf, 1983.

Burnham, Sophy. *A Book of Angels*. New York: Ballantine Books, 1990.

Davidson, Gustav. *A Dictionary of Angels*. New York: The Free Press, 1967.

Doyle, Sir Arthur Conan. *The History of Spiritualism*. 2 vols. New York: George H. Doran Co., 1926.

Doyle, Sir Arthur Conan. *Wanderings of a Spiritualist*. New York: George H. Doran Co., 1921.

Enoch. *The Book of Enoch or Enoch I*. Edited and translated by R. H. Charles. Oxford: Oxford University Press, 1912.

Evans, Hilary. *Gods, Spirits, Cosmic Guardians*. Wellingborough: The Aquarian Press, 1987.

Evans, Hilary. *Visions, Apparitions, Alien Visitors*. Wellingborough: The Aquarian Press, 1984.

Findhorn Community. *The Findhorn Garden*. London: Turnstone Books and Wildwood House Limited, 1976.

Freeman, Eileen Elias. *Touched by Angels*. New York: Warner Books, Inc., 1993.

Freeman, Eileen Elias. *Angelic Healing*. New York: Warner Books, Inc., 1994.

Georgian, Linda. *Your Guardian Angels*. New York: Simon and Schuster, 1994.

Gilmore, G. Don. *Angels, Angels, Everywhere*. New York: The Pilgrim Press, 1981.

Giovetti, Paola. *Angels: The Role of Celestial Guardians and Beings of Light*. York Beach: Samuel Weiser, Inc., 1993.

Goble, Eileen. *Spirit Guides*. Melbourne: The Holistic Centre, 1995.

Godwin, Malcolm. *Angels: An Endangered Species*. New York: Simon and Schuster, 1990.

Graham, Billy. *Angels: God's Secret Agents*. Waco: Word Inc., 1986.

Guiley, Rosemary Ellen. *Angels of Mercy*. New York: Pocket Books, 1994.

Hodson, Geoffrey. *The Coming of the Angels*. London: Rider and Company, 1932; Largs, Scotland: The Banton Press, 1993.

Hodson, Geoffrey. *The Kingdom of the Gods*. Adyar: The Theosophical Publishing House, 1952.

Howard, Jane M. *Commune With the Angels*. Virginia Beach: A.R.E. Press, 1992.

Josipovici, Gabriel. *The Book of God*. New Haven and London: Yale University Press, 1988.

Leadbeater, Charles W. *Invisible Helpers*. Adyar: The Theosophical Publishing House, 1928.

Maclean, Dorothy. *To Hear the Angels Sing*. Issaquah: Lorian Press, 1980.

McLean, Adam, ed. *A Treatise on Angel Magic*. Grand Rapids: Phanes Press, 1990.

Maskelyne, John Nevil. *Modern Spiritualism*. London: Frederick Warne and Company, 1876.

Moody, Dr. Raymond A. *Life After Life*. St. Simon's Island: Mockingbird Books, 1975.

Newhouse, Flower A. *Rediscovering the Angels*. Escondido: The Christward Ministry, 1950.

Newhouse, Flower A. *Flower A. Newhouse's Angels of Nature*. Wheaton: Quest Books, 1995.

Parente, Fr. Alessio. *Send Me Your Guardian Angels, Padre Pio*. Foggia: Editions, 1984.

Price, Hope. *Angels: True Stories of How They Touch Our Lives*. London: Macmillan London, 1993.

Price, John Randolph. *The Angels Within Us*. New York: Fawcett Columbine, 1993.

Ranke-Heinemann, Uta. *Putting Away Childish Things*. San Francisco: HarperSanFrancisco, 1994.

RavenWolf, Silver. *Angels: Companions in Magick.* St. Paul: Llewellyn Publications, 1996.

Roman, Sanaya and Packer, Duane. *Opening to Channel.* Tiburon: H. J. Kramer Inc., 1987.

Ronner, John. *Do You Have a Guardian Angel?* Murfreesboro: Mamre Press, 1985.

Ryerson, Kevin, and Stephanie Harolde. *Spirit Communication.* New York: Bantam Books, 1989.

Skultans, Vieda. *Intimacy and Ritual: A Study of Spiritualism, Mediums and Groups.* London: Routledge and Kegan Paul, 1974.

Smith, Robert C. *In the Presence of Angels.* Virginia Beach: A.R.E. Press, 1993.

Southern Centre of Theosophy, comp. *Devas and Men.* Adyar: The Theosophical Publishing House, 1977.

Steiner, Rudolf. *The Four Seasons and the Archangels.* London: Rudolf Steiner Press, 1947.

Swedenborg, Emanuel. *Heaven and Hell.* Translated by George F. Dole. New York: Swedenborg Foundation, Inc., 1976.

Taylor, Terry Lynn. *Messengers of Light.* Tiburon: H. J. Kramer, Inc., 1990.

Vance, Bruce A. *Mindscape.* Wheaton: Quest Books, 1990.

Webber, Marilynn Carlson, and William D. Webber. *A Rustle of Angels*. Grand Rapids: Zondervan Publishing House, 1994.

Wilson, Peter Lamborn. *Angels: Messengers of the Gods*. London: Thames and Hudson Limited, 1980.

Index

A

B

C

F

G

K

L

M

N

O

P

ORDER LLEWELLYN BOOKS TODAY!

Llewellyn publishes hundreds of books on your favorite subjects! To get these exciting books, including the ones on the following pages, check your local bookstore or order them directly from Llewellyn.

Order Online:
Visit our website at www.llewellyn.com, select your books, and order them on our secure server.

Order by Phone:

- Call toll-free within the U.S. at 1-877-NEW-WRLD (1-877-639-9753). Call toll-free within Canada at 1-866-NEW-WRLD (1-866-639-9753)
- We accept VISA, MasterCard, and American Express

Order by Mail:
Send the full price of your order (MN residents add 7% sales tax) in U.S. funds, plus postage & handling to:

Llewellyn Worldwide
P.O. Box 64383, Dept. 1-56718-795-1
St. Paul, MN 55164-0383, U.S.A.

Postage & Handling:

Standard (U.S., Mexico, & Canada). If your order is:
Up to $25.00, add $3.50
$25.01 - $48.99, add $4.00
$49.00 and over, FREE STANDARD SHIPPING
(Continental U.S. orders ship UPS. AK, HI, PR, & P.O. Boxes ship USPS 1st class. Mex. & Can. ship PMB.)

International Orders:

Surface Mail: For orders of $20.00 or less, add $5 plus $1 per item ordered. For orders of $20.01 and over, add $6 plus $1 per item ordered.

Air Mail:
Books: Postage & Handling is equal to the total retail price of all books in the order.
Non-book items: Add $5 for each item.

Orders are processed within 2 business days. Please allow for normal shipping time. Postage and handling rates subject to change.

Feng Shui for Beginners

Successful Living by Design

Richard Webster

Not advancing fast enough in your career? Maybe your desk is located in a "negative position." Wish you had a more peaceful family life? Hang a mirror in your dining room and watch what happens. Is money flowing out of your life rather than into it? You may want to look to the construction of your staircase!

For thousands of years, the ancient art of feng shui has helped people harness universal forces and lead lives rich in good health, wealth and happiness. The basic techniques in Feng Shui for Beginners are very simple, and you can put them into place immediately in your home and work environments. Gain peace of mind, a quiet confidence, and turn adversity to your advantage with feng shui remedies.

1-56718-803-6, 240 pp., 5¼ x 8,
photos, diagrams, softcover $12.95

To order, call 1–877-NEW WRLD

Prices subject to change without notice